Financial Discipleship

Building a Biblical Worldview of Money

Dr. Justin M. Henegar, Ph.D., CFP®, ChFC®, CKA®

For information contact: Dr. Justin M. Henegar at www.lextinwealth.com

Edited by: Debbie Philpott, Ed.D.
Cover Design: Jacob "Israel" Blackburn
Interior Design: Daniela Richardson

ISBN: 987-1-7325436-0-7
First Edition: 2018

10 9 8 7 6 5 4 3 2 1

DEDICATION

To my beloved wife Lexi
and all my wonderful and precious children:
Jaylyn, Jaxon, Ellie, Adley, Cora, Brynlee, and Thea

I love you all!

TABLE OF CONTENTS

QUICK TAB REFERENCE

INTRODUCTION

Discipleship may be defined as the process whereby an individual who has accepted a set of doctrines teaches those doctrines to others. For Christians, we find this call most prominent in the Gospel of Matthew where Jesus delivers his final earthly declaration.

> 'All authority in heaven and on earth has been given to me. Go therefore and make disciples of all nations, baptizing them in the name of the Father and of the Son and of the Holy Spirit, teaching them to observe all that I have commanded you; and lo, I am with you always, to the end of the age.' (Matt. 28:18-20)

In this declaration, Jesus gives his followers their objective: to baptize and to teach what they had been commanded by the Lord. In this, we are to know that Jesus will be with us as we seek to fulfill his command. This book is designed to help you to teach others the biblical principles and commands given to us by and through Christ. More specifically, this study will focus on the aspects of our attitude toward money, wealth, and materialism. Jesus told us that "Where your treasure is, there your heart will be also" (Matt. 6:21, NIV). Where is our treasure? The aim of this book is to help bring God's Word to life as we explore the transition of developing an appropriate worldview of money, wealth, and materialism.

With the guidance of the Holy Spirit, this book is designed to teach the most important aspect of learning about money, which, for most of us, was never taught to us or we never took the time to learn it. So you ask, "What is the most important part of learning about money?" In my opinion, we miss the opportunity about how our worldview affects the way we interact with money. Establishing our worldview about money may seem irrelevant, but the reality holds that financial management is no more than a process of decision making related to financial resources. The decisions we make, however, come from the way we see the world. Why do people save and others spend everything? Why do we borrow for a car rather than delay our gratification and save for a car? These types of questions come back to our worldview and belief system.

My hope is that by reading through this book, you will be able to learn, teach, and disciple the biblical truths regarding money and possessions. You see, we need to know, understand, and act in accordance with what God's Word says about money, so that God's truth will be the foundation of how and why we use money in the ways we do.

There are also several opportunities throughout this book to share the gospel message and allow the Holy Spirit to begin to work. My hope is that the Q&As will provide ample opportunity for Christian witness—for individuals to talk openly with others (or to learn for the first time for themselves) what it means to repent and believe the word, work, and worth of Jesus Christ.

Thank you for taking the time to invest in understanding what it means to be a steward of God's resources. Many blessings to you.

Justin

A CLASSICAL APPROACH TO FINANCIAL COMPETENCY

Before providing implementation strategies, it would be best to comment briefly on the importance of repetition in learning. For many of us, in order to truly learn something we need to be exposed to it multiple times. This is the general approach to classical education models. In short, in a classical education model a student is exposed to a topic (in our case, this would be God's perspective on finances) three times: 1) the grammar phase, 2) the logic phase, and 3) the rhetoric phase. The *grammar* phase involves teaching and memorizing the facts, definitions, general concepts, etc. In this level of learning, we are not learning the "why" yet but merely memorizing concepts. We then transition into the *logic* phase where the concepts learned in the grammar phase are put together to explain the why behind something. This area is where one can begin to support and explain the world in which they live. Finally, there is transition to the *rhetoric* phase. In this final phase, one is now tasked with supporting and defending their own thoughts and ideas on the topic.

CLASSICAL APPROACH TO BIBLICAL FINANCE

When applying the classical approach of learning to financial literacy or financial competency, it will build on itself such that the approach might look like the following:

Grammar Phase – Learning general concepts and definitions. This book would be the foundation of this phase, as a catechism approach seeks to teach and train through simple memorization of questions and answers.

Logic Phase – Here, one begins to see how biblical finance concepts are connected. Case studies may be used to explain why a biblical approach to money works and how a biblical approach may be applied.

Rhetoric Phase – In this final phase, the student begins to build a case for themselves and is able to defend and support their own understanding of biblical finance. Students are able to make biblical finance a part of who they are.

Using the classical approach, students are able to make biblical finance a part of who they are by establishing a financial worldview based on biblical principles.

HOW TO USE THIS BOOK

This book can be used in a variety of ways. It was written with a number of distinct study sessions in mind.

As with most catechism style books, much can be gained by simply starting your study with just the question and answer sections. This will accomplish two main goals: 1) it will help you learn what God has to say about money, and 2) the process will build memorization skills. With a total of 52 questions and answers, the study can easily be fitted to a year-long timetable by learning one question/answer per week.

A number of additional, distinct study sessions have also been identified. Whether you are completing the study individually, in pairs or as a couple, as a family, or within a small group, you are sure to find a method of study that will fit your schedule.

INDIVIDUAL DEVOTIONAL

If you plan to study financial discipleship by yourself—in solitude, with only the presence of the Holy Spirit guiding your thoughts— this resource will be uplifting and encouraging. Allowing the Holy

Spirit to work within you as you develop sound doctrine according to God's perspective on money can be life changing.

This book has five main sections: Question and Answer, Memorization Verse and Supporting Verses, Thoughts to Consider, Bible Study and Bible Study Questions. Each of the 52 lessons may be reviewed and studied in one setting or they may be divided within a single day or throughout the week. A few options include:

- *Daily Devotional.* Complete the reading and questions in one sitting. As a morning devotional, the daily review gives you the opportunity to reflect on the study throughout your day.

- *Daily Devotional with Split Study.* Perhaps you are stretched for time and desire to start your morning off with a few minutes of a devotional. Begin your day with the financial topic Question and Answer, Memorization Verse and Supporting Scripture, and Thoughts to Consider, reflecting on the new concepts and learning. Then, sometime during the day—perhaps during a lunch hour or in the evening—complete the remainder of the study.

- *Weekly Devotional.* On the first day of the week, read the Question and Answer, Memorization Verse, Scripture Support, and Thoughts to Consider for one question. Then select a day to complete the Bible Study. Answer the Bible Study Questions immediately following your Bible reading or return to the study on a different day to assess your memory and comprehension of the biblical passage. There can be great benefit to returning to the same question and answer throughout the week to explore not only the financial competency that will be developed but also to dive deep into God's Word and develop a more robust Bible acumen. Journaling would be a great spiritual discipline to incorporate with your week-long devotional.

COUPLES

Perhaps you are dating or have made your vows official and are married and want to build and establish an appropriate view of money. This resource will open up so many conversations that will help keep both of you accountable—not only to each other, as it relates to money decisions—but also to God as you build a new appreciation for what it means to be stewards. This resource can help each of you to draw closer to God and ultimately to one another in the process. It might be helpful to spend time going through each question and answer separately and then using a quiet evening (or date night) to study the Bible Study Questions together. Talk about your perspectives and how each question and answer has revealed something about you that might not have been considered previously.

SMALL GROUPS

If you are involved in a small group and searching for a topical Bible study, this resource could be exactly what you need. What better way than to establish a transparent way of talking about God's perspective on one of the most important topics of our life: money. A small group can use this resource by going through the Bible Study and Bible Study Questions every time they meet. The study can easily be divided into a year-long weekly study of the 52 Questions and Answers or into a shorter study by addressing all the Questions and Answers within each of the 12 subtopics. Group members can share what the Holy Spirit is leading in their life as it relates to each. It will be important to note that our money behaviors can be a very sensitive subject, so please be mindful of each person's willingness to share, or not share. Each member of the group should be extremely supportive of the others and remember that, together, you are learning God's Word about money which can be a phenomenal journey!

PARENTS

Another method for study could be parents taking their children through this book to teach a biblical worldview of money. The process of teaching financial literacy is a conversation that usually revolves around financial programs and initiatives structured within a school setting. However, if we delay the conversation start until a child reaches school age, then we may have completely missed our opportunity to help them establish an appropriate worldview of money.

If we do teach financial processes at home with our children, a typical approach is to start by putting three jars or envelopes out and having our children put money they receive into their "giving," "saving," and "spending" jars. This process continues until they are old enough to open a savings account at your local bank and then all the money goes into this new interest-bearing account. Finally, our children grow up and start working their first job which prompts them to open a checking account to include checks and debit cards. Viola, they are now set to take on managing money and all that entails. However, while the threefold approach is better than no approach at all, it is limited in helping them to gain true biblical wisdom on financial matters.

When starting this study, if you have children that fall within a wide range of ages, you may decide to go through each Q&A with the entire family and have the younger kids only do the Q&A. The middle kids can memorize the Scripture Support in addition to the Q&A, while the oldest kids should be encouraged to complete all sections: Question and Answer, Memorization Verse, Scripture Support, Thoughts to Consider and Bible Study Questions.

A NOTE TO PARENTS

Did you know that it is our responsibility as parents and stewards of what God has entrusted to us to teach our children the Word of Truth? The Bible gives us ample instruction as devoted followers of Christ:

- **Proverbs 22:6**: *Train up a child in the way he should go; even when he is old he will not depart from it.*

- **Ephesians 6:4:** *Fathers, do not provoke your children to anger, but bring them up in the discipline and instruction of the Lord.*

- **Deuteronomy 6:6–7:** *And these words that I command you today shall be on your heart. You shall teach them diligently to your children, and shall talk of them when you sit in your house, and when you walk by the way, and when you lie down, and when you rise.*

- **3 John 1:4:** *I have no greater joy than to hear that my children are walking in the truth.*

- **Proverbs 6:20–21:** *My son, keep your father's commandment, and forsake not your mother's teaching. Bind them on your heart always; tie them around your neck.*

- **Proverbs 3:1:** *My son, do not forget my teaching, but let your heart keep my commandments.*

- **Romans 12:1–2:** *I appeal to you therefore, brothers, by the mercies of God, to present your bodies as a living sacrifice, holy and acceptable to God, which is your spiritual worship. Do not be conformed to this world, but be transformed by the renewal of your mind, that by testing you may discern what is the will of God, what is good and acceptable and perfect.*

- **Proverbs 20:11:** *Even a child makes himself known by his acts, by whether his conduct is pure and upright.*

- **Genesis 18:19:** *"For I have chosen him, that he may command his children and his household after him to keep the way of the Lord by doing righteousness and justice, so that the Lord may bring Abraham what he has promised him."*

WHY WORLDVIEW IS SO IMPORTANT

Before diving into the array of questions throughout this book, it is important to fully understand the need to develop a biblical worldview, especially as it relates to money. Although this may be known intuitively, we often don't think about the implications of what makes up our worldview or how our worldview drives EVERY decision we make. Worldview might be defined as:

1. the foundation and basis from which individuals make all of their decisions,

2. a set of core beliefs that make up one's self identity and convictions about the world, or

3. the way someone thinks about the world.

So, what makes up our worldview? The answer is everything, really. Our beliefs/faith, past experiences, the way we were raised, our education, peer influence, and culture—all of these influences shape the way we interpret the world in which we live. Although much more could be said about worldview, for this study it is important to have a broad understanding of what it is and how to make known those core beliefs or values that may lie in our subconscious but significantly impact each and every decision we make.

As you go through this book, stop and ask yourself or partner, your small group, or even your children, the questions that follow in order to begin to understand what is contributing to each one's understanding of the financial discipleship questions and answers. As you complete this study, return to the list of questions often to increase your awareness of differing worldviews and to more fully develop your own. The questions shown below can also be used as great conversation starters for a more insightful discussion of the financial topics.

Questions to better understand the *nature* of our current beliefs— what they are and how we have come to accept them as our own:

1. What comes to mind when I first think about this question and answer?

2. What experience have I had that relates to this question and answer?

3. What have I previously been taught related to this question and answer? Is what I was taught *in accordance with* or *contrary to* the biblical principles identified in this book?

4. How would my parents (grandparents) react to the question?

5. How would my co-workers/colleagues at work react to this question and answer? What would be their response?

6. How would society react to this question and answer? Would I agree or disagree with their reaction?

7. What would hold me back or is holding me back from accepting this as truth, if anything?

**Note to Parents: As a general guideline, these questions are probably most appropriate for children over the age of 13.

God's Ownership

Question 1:

What does God own?

ANSWER:

God owns everything, the Earth, and
everything in it.

 MEMORY VERSE

PSALM 24:1

*The earth is the Lord's, and the fullness thereof, the world,
and those who dwell therein,*

SCRIPTURE SUPPORT

Genesis 14:19: *And he blessed Abram, saying, "Blessed be Abram by God
Most High, Creator of heaven and earth."*

Deuteronomy 10:14: *Behold, to the Lord your God belong heaven and the
heaven of heavens, the earth with all that is in it.*

1 Chronicles 29:11–12: *Yours, O Lord, is the greatness and the power
and the glory and the victory and the majesty, for all that is in the heavens and
in the earth is yours. Yours is the kingdom, O Lord, and you are exalted as head
above all. Both riches and honor come from you, and you rule over all. In your
hand are power and might, and in your hand it is to make great and to give
strength to all.*

THOUGHTS TO CONSIDER

God created everything; everything is his to do with what he wants. As we think about the things we have such as our toys, electronics, and even our money, it all belongs to God. This is the most fundamental truth that we need to know and understand as it relates to having a biblical view of money and using our money to God's glory.

BIBLE STUDY

Deuteronomy 10:12–22

BIBLE STUDY QUESTIONS

1. What five things does God require of his people?

2. Although God owns everything, what did God do?

3. How does Deuteronomy 10:14 inform our understanding of what God is asking for in verse 10:16 when he tells the Israelites to circumcise their hearts and to no longer be stiffnecked?

4. What does God do to those who have very little (i.e., fatherless, widow, sojourner)?

5. Knowing that God owns everything, what are we to do for sojourners?

6. How does having a perspective that God owns everything change our thoughts about money?

Answers: Page 165

Question 2:

If God owns everything, what is our role?

ANSWER:

We are to act as stewards of what God gives us.

 MEMORY VERSE

PSALM 8:6

You have given him dominion over the works of your hand; you have put all things under his feet,

SCRIPTURE SUPPORT

Genesis 1:28: *And God blessed them. And God said to them, "Be fruitful and multiply and fill the earth and subdue it, and have dominion over the fish of the sea and over the birds of the heavens and over every living thing that moves on the earth."*

Psalm 115:16: *The heavens are the Lord's heavens, but the earth he has given to the children of man.*

Luke 12:42: *And the Lord said, "Who then is the faithful and wise manager, whom his master will set over his household, to give them their portion of food at the proper time?"*

THOUGHTS TO CONSIDER

A steward is someone who handles or manages another person's belongs. This can be an easy concept to understand but extremely challenging in its implementation. If you were to show someone everything that God has blessed you with, and given you responsibility over, would you say, "Look, here is *my...*" or, would you say, "Look, God has allowed me to manage...".? Once we start recognizing that everything is the Lord's, the way we manage his resources is significantly different than how we would manage "our" resources.

**Note to Parents: An example of stewardship that you can share with your child is about their borrowing a toy from a friend. *"When a friend allows you to use their toys or belongings, you do not own that toy, but you are given the opportunity to use it. That is the same thing with God. Since he owns everything, he puts us in a position to take care of what he created."*

BIBLE STUDY

Genesis 39:1-6

BIBLE STUDY QUESTIONS

1. Who are the main characters?

2. How did Potiphar view Joseph?

3. Based on how Potiphar viewed Joseph, what did he do?

4. Once Potiphar put Joseph in charge of his household, how did Potiphar feel?

5. Think about a time when you were allowed to use something that belonged to someone else. How did you handle what you were given? If you handled it differently, why?

Answers: Page 167

Question 3:

How do we become a biblical steward?

> **ANSWER:**
>
> We must first give up ownership of our possessions through repentance and faith in Christ Jesus.

 MEMORY VERSE

LUKE 14:33

"So therefore, any one of you who does not renounce all that he has cannot be my disciple."

SCRIPTURE SUPPORT

Matthew 19:27–29: *Then Peter said in reply, "See, we have left everything and followed you. What then will we have?" Jesus said to them, "Truly, I say to you, in the new world, when the Son of Man will sit on his glorious throne, you who have followed me will also sit on twelve thrones, judging the twelve tribes of Israel. And everyone who has left houses or brothers or sisters or father or mother or children or lands, for my name's sake, will receive a hundredfold and will inherit eternal life.*

Mark 10:28–30: *Peter began to say to him, "See, we have left everything and followed you." Jesus said, "Truly, I say to you, there is no one who has left house or brothers or sisters or mother or father or children or lands, for my sake and for the gospel, who will not receive a hundredfold now in this time, houses and brothers and sisters and mothers and children and lands, with persecutions, and in the age to come eternal life."'*

1 Corinthians 4:1–2: *This is how one should regard us, as servants of Christ and stewards of the mysteries of God. Moreover, it is required of stewards that they be found faithful.*

THOUGHTS TO CONSIDER

This question should probably read, "How do I accept Christ as my Lord and Savior?" Before we can really think biblically about money, we need to know Christ as our Lord, our provider, and our counselor. We can do this by repenting of our sin and realizing that only through Christ can we be reconciled back to God our Father.

This question will not have the Bible Study or Bible Study Questions sections which are replaced with Bible Verses and Prayer to help guide you, your family, and or friends to hear the Word of God in anticipation that the Holy Spirit will help one and all to realize our total depravity and need for a savior.

BIBLE VERSES

Romans 3:23: *for all have sinned and fall short of the glory of God,*

Romans 6:23: *For the wages of sin is death, but the free gift of God is eternal life in Christ Jesus our Lord.*

Romans 5:8: *But God demonstrates His own love toward us, in that while we were yet sinners, Christ died for us.*

John 3:16: *"For God so loved the world, that He gave His only begotten Son, that whoever believes in Him shall not perish, but have eternal life."*

Romans 10:9: *that if you confess with your mouth Jesus as Lord, and believe in your heart that God raised Him from the dead, you will be saved;*

1 John 1:9: *If we confess our sins, He is faithful and righteous to forgive us our sins and to cleanse us from all unrighteousness.*

John 1:12: *But as many as received Him, to them He gave the right to become children of God, even to those who believe in His name,*

Ephesians 2:8–9: *For by grace you have been saved through faith; and that not of yourselves, it is the gift of God; not as a result of works, so that no one may boast.*

2 Corinthians 5:17: *Therefore if anyone is in Christ, he is a new creature; the old things passed away; behold, new things have come.*

Ephesians 1:7: *In Him we have redemption through His blood, the forgiveness of our trespasses, according to the riches of His grace.*

Prayer

Heavenly Father,

May your Word rest upon us as we read these verses. May the act of hearing your words prompt us to acknowledge that we are sinners and have rebelled against your perfect ways. You, and you alone, provide new mercies and grace each day through our new and revitalized faith in your son, Christ Jesus. For as we read, it was by his death and your gift of grace—not by our works—that allows us to be called your children, heirs with Christ, your son.

Lord, we pray that those reciting (and hearing) this prayer accept and acknowledge we are all sinners and have need to repent, to turn away from our sinful nature, and believe in the work and worth of Jesus Christ. Allow the Holy Spirit to lead us each day as we strive to know you more, seek the things of your divine nature, and become a new creature. May this book be used as a tool to continually guide us to repentance and faith in Christ.

Amen.

Question 4:

When does becoming a steward take effect?

ANSWER:

We become stewards when we accept and follow Jesus Christ.

 MEMORY VERSE

Matthew 16:24

Then Jesus said to his disciples, "Whoever wants to be my disciple must deny themselves and take up their cross and follow me."

SCRIPTURE SUPPORT

1 Peter 2:21: *For to this you have been called, because Christ also suffered for you, leaving you an example, so that you might follow in his steps.*

John 10:27: *"My sheep hear my voice, and I know them, and they follow me."*

Luke 5:27–28: *After this he went out and saw a tax collector named Levi, sitting at the tax booth. And he said to him, "Follow me." And leaving everything, he rose and followed him.*

THOUGHTS TO CONSIDER

Jesus tells us that we must deny ourselves, take up our cross, and follow him. We cannot follow our own desires and follow Christ at the same time. The concept of biblical stewardship starts when we accept this command from Christ—to deny ourselves and to follow him. Once we acknowledge who God is and what God has done for us, our worldview should change. We begin to see God as the owner. Our role is to glorify him in all we do, especially with how we take care of what he has given us.

BIBLE STUDY
Matthew 16:21–28

BIBLE STUDY QUESTIONS

1. What was Jesus' response to Simon Peter when he tried to rebuke him?

2. When we think that we own our material possessions, are our thoughts on the things of God or the things of man? Why?

3. How can we transition from thinking about the things of man to thinking about the things of God?

4. As you think about God's ownership of all that you possess, do you feel that you have relinquished ownership of your possessions?

Answers: Page 168

Question 5:

What does a steward receive for their work?

ANSWER:

A faithful steward will be blessed with more responsibility.

 MEMORY VERSE

MATTHEW 25:21

"His master said to him, 'Well done, good and faithful servant. You have been faithful over a little; I will set you over much. Enter into the joy of your master.'"

SCRIPTURE SUPPORT

1 Corinthians 4:2: *Moreover, it is required of stewards that they be found faithful.*

Proverbs 28:20: *A faithful man will abound with blessings, but whoever hastens to be rich will not go unpunished.*

John 3:27: *John answered, "A person cannot receive even one thing unless it is given him from heaven."*

THOUGHTS TO CONSIDER

The concept of blessing generates confusion within the Christian community. For many, when the word *blessed* is used, there is a cultural connotation suggesting financially blessed: however, it means "to make holy or consecrate." With this definition in mind, it makes sense that when we act as a steward of God's possessions, and use them according to his will, that he would bless us or make us holy. Our ultimate goal is to become like Christ, to be considered righteous before God. To have God say to us, *"Well done, good and faithful servant! You have been faithful with a few things; I will put you in charge of many things. Come and share your master's happiness!"* (Matt. 25:23).

BIBLE STUDY
Genesis 22

BIBLE STUDY QUESTIONS

1. Who are the characters in this story?

2. What did God ask Abraham to do?

3. When did Abraham act on the task commanded by God?

4. Refer to Genesis 22:10. Why was Abraham's response to God's command so important in light of being a steward?

5. Reread Genesis 22:15–18. What did the Lord say (and do) to Abraham?

Answers: Page 170

Stewardship

Question 6:

How do we get the things we have?

ANSWER:

Everything comes from the Lord.

 MEMORY VERSE

ROMANS 11:36

*For from him and through him and for him are all things.
To him be the glory forever! Amen.*

SCRIPTURE SUPPORT

1 Chronicles 29:14: *"But who am I, and what is my people, that we should be able thus to offer willingly? For all things come from you, and of your own have we given you."*

1 Timothy 6:17: *As for the rich in this present age, charge them not to be haughty, nor to set their hopes on the uncertainty of riches, but on God, who richly provides us with everything to enjoy.*

Philippians 4:19: *And my God will supply all your needs according to His riches in glory in Christ Jesus.*

THOUGHTS TO CONSIDER

As we have seen, God owns everything. Everything is his. And since he owns everything, God can give us what he desires, not always what we want. Being mindful that God is the owner, we should be in constant thanksgiving that he has given to us the things we currently have because it is by his grace we have them. That said, our God is a giving God and we are to make our requests known to him (Phil. 4:6).

BIBLE STUDY
Matthew 6:19–34

BIBLE STUDY QUESTIONS

1. What does Jesus instruct us to do in the first part of his monologue?

2. What specific emotion is addressed by Jesus?

3. What reason does Jesus offer the audience to assure them of provision?

4. What does Jesus say the Gentiles seek after?

5. What does Jesus say that Christians should seek after?

Answers: Page 172

Question 7:

How much does God give us?

ANSWER:

God gives us exactly what we need to glorify him.

 MEMORY VERSE

MATTHEW 25:14–15

"For it will be like a man going on a journey, who called his servants and entrusted to them his property. To one he gave five talents, to another two, to another one, to each according to his ability. Then he went away."

SCRIPTURE SUPPORT

2 Samuel 12:7–8: *Nathan said to David, "You are the man! Thus says the Lord, the God of Israel, 'I anointed you king over Israel, and I delivered you out of the hand of Saul. And I gave you your master's house and your master's wives into your arms and gave you the house of Israel and of Judah. And if this were too little, I would add to you as much more.'"*

John 3:16: *"For God so loved the world, that he gave his only Son, that whoever believes in him should not perish but have eternal life."*

Romans 8:32: *He who did not spare his own Son but gave him up for us all, how will he not also with him graciously give us all things?*

THOUGHTS TO CONSIDER

God wants us to praise and worship him, although he gives us a choice to do so. When we submit, and commit our lives to Christ, we begin to realize that God will give us exactly what we need to praise and worship him. This may come from not having very little and being humble in our ways, or having an abundance of financial resources in which we are ever grateful. God deserves glory and honor no matter our circumstances.

BIBLE STUDY
Luke 9:1-6, 22:35-37

BIBLE STUDY QUESTIONS

1. What is happening at this point in Jesus' ministry?

2. What did Jesus give to his disciples before he sent them out?

3. After Jesus gave the disciples authority, what did he command them to take?

4. Why did Jesus not allow the disciples to take any necessities or money to buy necessities on their journey?

5. Refer to Luke 22:35–37. What did Jesus ask the disciples? What was their response?

6. Do you believe that we must first go through a faith strengthening exercise like that of the disciples before we can use God's resources and keep our stronghold faith?

Answers: Page 174

Question 8:

If we trust in God, will he financially bless us?

ANSWER:

God will provide us with what he desires.

 MEMORY VERSE

1 SAMUEL 2:7

The Lord makes poor and makes rich; he brings low and he exalts.

SCRIPTURE SUPPORT

Ecclesiastes 7:14: *In the day of prosperity be joyful, and in the day of adversity consider: God has made the one as well as the other, so that man may not find out anything that will be after him.*

Psalm 37:4: *Delight yourself in the Lord, and he will give you the desires of your heart.*

Luke 16:10: *"One who is faithful in a very little is also faithful in much, and one who is dishonest in a very little is also dishonest in much."*

THOUGHTS TO CONSIDER

Remember that God owns everything and he has the ability to give each person what he desires. Unfortunately, for many of us, we expect that by trusting in God he will make us prosperous or financially bless us in some way. If we believe that, we may have a misguided view of who God is. Remember that Jesus took on the role of humankind, humbled himself, and became a servant. As you may recall, Jesus replied, *"Foxes have dens and birds have nests, but the Son of Man has no place to lay his head"* (Matt. 8:20). If Christ was humbled with very little, we can expect God to allow us the same privilege.

BIBLE STUDY
1 Kings 17:7-16

BIBLE STUDY QUESTIONS

1. Who are the characters in 1 Kings 17:7–16?

2. Where did God command Elijah to go and what was Elijah expecting to receive when he got there?

3. What was the widow's reply to Elijah when he asked her to bring him a piece of bread?

4. What was Elijah's response to her?

5. What did Elijah say to the widow on behalf of the Lord?

6. Even though the widow had only enough for one last meal, what do you think inspired her to do what Elijah said, knowing her circumstances were so dire?

Answers: Page 175

Question 9:

Can God take away what he has given us?

> **ANSWER:**
>
> Yes, since God owns everything, he can give and take away.

 MEMORY VERSE

JOB 1:21–22

And he said, "Naked I came from my mother's womb, and naked shall I return. The Lord gave, and the Lord has taken away; blessed be the name of the Lord." In all this Job did not sin or charge God with wrong.

SCRIPTURE SUPPORT

Proverbs 15:25: *The Lord tears down the house of the proud but maintains the widow's boundaries.*

Luke 12:22–26: *And he said to his disciples, "Therefore I tell you, do not be anxious about your life, what you will eat, nor about your body, what you will put on. For life is more than food, and the body more than clothing. Consider the ravens: they neither sow nor reap, they have neither storehouse nor barn, and yet God feeds them. Of how much more value are you than the birds! And which of you by being anxious can add a single hour to his span of life? If then you are not able to do as small a thing as that, why are you anxious about the rest?"*

Psalm 135:6: *Whatever the Lord pleases, he does, in heaven and on earth, in the seas and all deeps.*

THOUGHTS TO CONSIDER

Most of us know that when we make a mistake there are consequences and, at times, those consequences result in the loss of a privilege or loss of material possessions. However, it is important that we also realize, as shared in the story of Job, that God has the ability to give and to take away at his discretion, which may not necessarily be tied to a "punishment" for our wrongdoing. This can only be understood when we discern that God owns everything.

**Note to Parents: Although this concept is not difficult to understand, it may be hard to explain to kids. One example you can provide to your children is when they ask to use something of yours. Suppose they want to play a game on your mobile phone or tablet. You may allow them at times to have access to your phone or tablet, but then you may decide to not allow them to play. You, as the owner, have the right to make that choice, just as God has the right to allow us access to his possessions and then not allow us to access them at other times.

BIBLE STUDY
Job 1:1-22

BIBLE STUDY QUESTIONS

1. What were some of the characteristics used to describe Job?

2. What was Job doing for his children after their feasts?

3. What reasons did Satan give to the Lord that justified Job's righteousness?

4. What did Satan suggest the Lord do that would make Job curse the Lord's name?

5. To prove Job's righteousness, what did the Lord allow Satan to do to him? Were there any conditions?

6. As you think about the first part of the story of Job, what is to be our attitude regarding what we have?

Answers: Page 177

Question 10:

What happens if we put our trust in money?

ANSWER:

If we put our trust in money, we are not putting our trust and faith in Jesus Christ.

 MEMORY VERSE

PROVERBS 11:28

Whoever trusts in his riches will fall, but the righteous will flourish like a green leaf.

SCRIPTURE SUPPORT

Luke 12:42–44: *And the Lord said, "Who then is the faithful and wise manager, whom his master will set over his household, to give them their portion of food at the proper time? Blessed is that servant whom his master will find so doing when he comes. Truly, I say to you, he will set him over all his possessions."*

Jeremiah 17:5–6: *Thus, says the Lord: "Cursed is the man who trusts in man and makes flesh his strength, whose heart turns away from the Lord. He is like a shrub in the desert, and shall not see any good come. He shall dwell in the parched places of the wilderness, in an uninhabited salt land."*

Ecclesiastes 5:10: *He who loves money will not be satisfied with money, nor he who loves wealth with his income; this also is vanity.*

THOUGHTS TO CONSIDER

Putting trust in money diverts our putting trust in God for provision of our needs. This concept can be the most challenging to accomplish. As our financial account balances grow, we can very easily not think to pray and seek God's direction on financial decisions in our life because we know we have the money. The more money we have, the easier it becomes to remove our dependence on God. This maybe one of the reasons Christ talks so much about coming for the poor, as they have nothing else to depend on.

**Note to Parents: This can be a challenging concept to grasp, especially for teens and young adults. We must heed the words of Christ when asked about the two greatest commands. Jesus replied: "'*Love the Lord your God with all your heart and with all your soul and with all your mind.*' This is the first and greatest commandment. And the second is like it: '*Love your neighbor as yourself.*' All the Law and the Prophets hang on these two commandments" (Matt. 22:37–40). When we put our trust in money, we are removing our trust in Christ and replacing him as our top priority, where we can no longer love him with ALL our heart, soul, and mind.

BIBLE STUDY

Acts 4:32-37

BIBLE STUDY QUESTIONS

1. What does Acts 4:32 tell us about the people?

2. What were these early Christians doing?

3. Ananias and Sapphira were the two main characters in Acts 5:1–11. What did they sell? Why?

4. What "little" thing did Ananias and Sapphira do?

5. While the Apostle Peter was talking to Ananias, what happened?

6. What happened when Sapphira came back to talk to Peter?

7. Do you feel that the death of Ananias and Sapphira was too extreme? Why or why not?

Answers: Page 180

Contentment

Question 11:

What is contentment?

ANSWER:

Contentment is a state of being completely satisfied by a dependence on God's provision for our sustainment.

MEMORY VERSE

PHILIPPIANS 4:11–13

Not that I am speaking of being in need, for I have learned in whatever situation I am to be content. I know how to be brought low, and I know how to abound. In any and every circumstance, I have learned the secret of facing plenty and hunger, abundance and need. I can do all things through him who strengthens me.

SCRIPTURE SUPPORT

Isaiah 41:13: *For I, the Lord your God, hold your right hand it is I who say to you, "Fear not, I am the one who helps you."*

Psalm 73:26: *My flesh and my heart may fail, but God is the strength of my heart and my portion forever.*

Psalm 121:1–2: *I lift up my eyes to the hills. From where does my help come? My help comes from the Lord, who made heaven and earth.*

THOUGHTS TO CONSIDER

The idea of *contentment* is one of the most challenging aspects of financial stewardship. Our natural tendency is to want and desire more than we have which can easily cause us to move away from confidently anticipating God will provide for our needs to a focus on how we can best provide for our own needs. Errantly, we displace God as provider and sustainer, and place ourselves in that role.

BIBLE STUDY

2 Corinthians 11:20–29

BIBLE STUDY QUESTIONS

1. Is Paul being bold? How do you know?

2. What characteristics does Paul emphasize about himself?

3. What punishments does Paul describe in his letter to the Corinthians?

4. In what year was 2 Corinthians thought to be written by Paul?

5. When was the letter to the Philippians written by Paul?

6. If Paul suffered the many perils he encountered before he wrote about learning to be *content*, how can we follow Paul's example?

Answers: Page 183

Question 12:

How are we to be content?

ANSWER:

We are to acknowledge that Christ is with us and will never leave nor forsake us.

MEMORY VERSE

HEBREWS 13:5

Keep your life free from love of money, and be content with what you have, for he has said, "I will never leave you nor forsake you."

SCRIPTURE SUPPORT

1 Timothy 6:6–7: *But godliness with contentment is great gain, for we brought nothing into the world, and we cannot take anything out of the world.*

Psalm 37:4: *Delight yourself in the Lord, and he will give you the desires of your heart.*

Matthew 6:33: *"But seek first the kingdom of God and his righteousness, and all these things will be added to you."*

THOUGHTS TO CONSIDER

As we know from our previous questions, we are to be content. However, always in question is "With how much should we be content?" The answer is very simple: what we have right now. You see, we are stewards and nothing is ours. We are in a role of responsibility to manage God's resources and, therefore, what God gives us to manage is rightfully his, not ours. God has the right to give to each person what he desires, and what he gives us is enough because God is always with us.

BIBLE STUDY
Romans 9

BIBLE STUDY QUESTIONS

1. Identify the main theme of Romans 9.

2. What major point is discussed in Romans 9:1–14?

3. What promise does Paul write about that was spoken by God to Moses?

4. What are the two challenging questions that man may ask God? What is Paul's response?

5. As you reflect on Romans 9, what do you think of the phrase, "It's not fair," when looking at what others have?

Answers: Page 185

Question 13:

How do we learn to be content?

ANSWER:

Contentment comes from desiring Christ.

 MEMORY VERSE

Psalm 73:25

Whom have I in heaven but you? And there is nothing on earth that I desire besides you.

SCRIPTURE SUPPORT

Isaiah 26:9: *My soul yearns for you in the night; my spirit within me earnestly seeks you. For when your judgments are in the earth, the inhabitants of the world learn righteousness.*

Psalm 119:81: *My soul longs for Your salvation; I hope in your word.*

Psalm 107:9: *For he satisfies the longing soul, and the hungry soul he fills with good things.*

THOUGHTS TO CONSIDER

By desiring Christ and following after him, he will provide us with many blessings in our life. From the previous Q&A, recall Paul's words: *"I can do all this through him who gives me strength"* (Phil. 4:13). But we must remember that these words come in the context of contentment. We will see this in the Bible Study.

**Note to Parents: This may be a challenging question and answer to discuss with your children, but it is imperative that they hear from you that desiring Christ should be our only desire. It is important that children understand the purpose of man, which is to praise, honor, and glorify God. This foundational Christian worldview sets the stage for how they will see the world and, more importantly, how their actions will reflect a strong desire to glorify God in all they do, especially the management of God's financial resources.

BIBLE STUDY
Philippians 4

BIBLE STUDY QUESTIONS

1. What does Paul ask of his readers in Philippians 4:1?

2. Who were the two individuals involved in a disagreement?

3. What did Paul ask the Philippians to do with the two having disagreement? Why?

4. Paul writes that we are not to be anxious about anything. How are we to do that?

5. What does Paul's advice bring?

6. Paul rejoices in the Philippians' concern over him, but he also understands what about the Philippians?

7. What has Paul learned about being in need?

8. What is the secret Paul was proclaiming?

9. How do two relatively separate issues— disagreeing and learning to live with little or with abundance—relate to contentment starting with desiring Christ?

Answers: Page 187

Question 14:

What happens when we are not content?

> **ANSWER:**
>
> A lack of contentment will spur worry and anxiety in our life.

 MEMORY VERSE

Luke 12:22

And he said to his disciples, "Therefore I tell you, do not be anxious about your life, what you will eat, nor about your body, what you will put on."

SCRIPTURE SUPPORT

Matthew 6:25–34: *"Therefore I tell you, do not be anxious about your life, what you will eat or what you will drink, nor about your body, what you will put on. Is not life more than food, and the body more than clothing? Look at the birds of the air: they neither sow nor reap nor gather into barns, and yet your heavenly Father feeds them. Are you not of more value than they? And which of you by being anxious can add a single hour to his span of life? And why are you anxious about clothing? Consider the lilies of the field, how they grow: they neither toil nor spin, yet I tell you, even Solomon in all his glory was not arrayed like one of these. But if God so clothes the grass of the field, which today is alive and tomorrow is thrown into the oven, will he not much more clothe you, O you of little faith? Therefore do not be anxious, saying, 'What shall we eat?' or 'What shall we drink?' or 'What shall we wear?' For the Gentiles seek after all these things, and your heavenly Father knows that you need them all. But seek first the kingdom of God and his righteousness, and all these things will be added to you. Therefore do not be anxious about tomorrow, for tomorrow will be anxious for itself. Sufficient for the day is its own trouble."*

John 14:27: *"Peace I leave with you; my peace I give you. I do not give to you as the world gives. Do not let your hearts be troubled and do not be afraid."*

1 Peter 5:6–8: *Humble yourselves, therefore, under God's mighty hand, that he may lift you up in due time. Cast all your anxiety on him because he cares for you. Be alert and of sober mind. Your enemy the devil prowls around like a roaring lion looking for someone to devour.*

THOUGHTS TO CONSIDER

When we lose our contentment (or perhaps we never had it), we tend to focus on what we don't have or what others have instead of us. This focus uses our energy and creates anxiety and worry. We use energy to think about how we can get what we don't have and this sense of planning can rob us of the peace and joy that is ours when we know and believe Christ Jesus as provider. Once we recognize that God knows all our needs—even before we prayerfully make our requests (Matt. 6:7-8), we will realize there is no need to worry about such things or to be discontent in our present situation.

BIBLE STUDY

Ecclesiastes 1–2

BIBLE STUDY QUESTIONS

1. Who wrote Ecclesiastes? What did he call himself?
2. What did Solomon say to himself in Ecclesiastes 1:1?
3. What was Solomon searching to find?
4. List the things that Solomon did to accomplish his goal?
5. Where did all the possessions put Solomon in the rank of wealth among men?
6. What did Solomon deny himself?
7. What was Solomon's ultimate conclusion?
8. According to Solomon, what comes to one who is not content?

Answers: Page 190

Question 15:

What makes us content?

┌─ ANSWER: ──────────────────────────────

We are made content by having our
basic needs meet.

└──

 ## MEMORY VERSE

1 TIMOTHY 6:8

*But if we have food and clothing, with these we will be
content.*

SCRIPTURE SUPPORT

Luke 12:24: *"Consider the ravens, they neither sow nor reap, they have neither
storehouses nor barn, and yet God feeds then. Of how much more value are you
than the birds."*

Psalm 23:1: *The Lord is my shepherd, I lack nothing.*

Philippians 4:19: *And my God will supply every need of yours according
to his riches in glory in Christ Jesus.*

THOUGHTS TO CONSIDER

As a steward, we acknowledge that God owns everything. In addition, we know that God loves us so much that he sent his son to die on a cross for us. These two facts (that he owns everything and he loves us) should assure us that God will provide for our needs. Unfortunately, he will not always give us what we want. This leads us to acknowledge that God has already given us what we have at this point and that it is sufficient (if it wasn't, he would have given us more). We need to trust in the fact that God gives us enough to glorify him in what we have.

BIBLE STUDY
Daniel 1:1–15

BIBLE STUDY QUESTIONS

1. During the time Daniel was written, who was King of Judah?
2. Who defeated King Jehoiakim?
3. What was the Lord's part in the battle between the two kings?
4. Who are the four main characters of Daniel 1? Give both of their names.
5. What were the characteristics of the four boys?
6. How were the youths to be treated?
7. What was Daniel's request?
8. What was the result of Daniel's request after the 10-day period?
9. What does the story of Daniel reveal about contentment with what God provides us?

Answers: Page 193

Question 16:

Should we be content with the money that we earn?

> **ANSWER:**
>
> Yes, we should be content with our wages.

 MEMORY VERSE

Luke 3:14

Soldiers also asked him, "And we, what shall we do?" And he said to them, "Do not extort money from anyone by threats or by false accusation, and be content with your wages."

SCRIPTURE SUPPORT

Hebrews 11:6: *And without faith it is impossible to please him, for whoever would draw near to God must believe that he exists and that he rewards those who seek him.*

1 Timothy 6:10: *For the love of money is a root of all kinds of evil. It is through this craving that some have wandered away from the faith and pierced themselves with many pangs.*

Proverbs 28:6: *Better is a poor man who walks in his integrity than a rich man who is crooked in his ways.*

THOUGHTS TO CONSIDER

One question we rarely hear asked, unless filling out an application of some sort, is "How much money do you make?" Since this is such a personal subject, it is usually kept confidential. However, it may also be to our benefit that earnings and wages of others are left unspoken. At some point, it is likely that we each have heard or found out what someone else makes. If the amount is higher than is subjectively felt they should be making, then our first reaction might be a sense of unfairness, injustice, or disgust. Why is this the case? It could be that we equate our earnings with our self-worth and when we learn what others make, we may immediately think less of ourselves. We might also place a higher value on our contributions in the workplace than we do others' contributions—whether realistic or not. So, the next time you hear "I just found out what Johnny makes?" Walk away! Be content with what you have and let God deal with what others have.

**Note to Parents: As kids progress from a child into the pre-teens and teenage years, they will quickly realize that people make different amounts of money. Their older siblings may get a larger allowance or receive more money for their birthday and perhaps see that their younger siblings get less money than they do. If your child doesn't see this, you may want to talk about the fact that each individual's situation is unique and because of these unique factors (personal experience, skill set, our attitude, and personality) we may get paid different amounts for our services. Whatever the amount, we need to know that God is providing this money as a way to provide for us and we need to be completely dependent on God to know how much we need.

BIBLE STUDY
1 Timothy 6

BIBLE STUDY QUESTIONS

1. What does Paul say about those who seek to constantly make more money?

2. What does Paul say is the root of all kinds of evils?

3. What does Paul's saying mean to us?

4. What happens if we fall into a desire to want more?

5. What is Paul's advice?

6. Why do you believe Paul asks us to flee the pursuit of desiring more money?

Answers: Page 195

Our Financial
Faithfulness

Question 17:

Can God use giving to test our faithfulness in him?

ANSWER:

Yes, God can use giving as a test of our faith.

 MEMORY VERSE

JAMES 2:14–17

What good is it, my brothers, if someone says he has faith but does not have works? Can that faith save him? If a brother or sister is poorly clothed and lacking in daily food, and one of you says to them, "Go in peace, be warmed and filled," without giving them the things needed for the body, what good is that? So also faith by itself, if it does not have works, is dead.

SCRIPTURE SUPPORT

Psalm 50:15: *"…and call upon me in the day of trouble; I will deliver you, and you shall glorify me."*

Jeremiah 17:7: *"Blessed is the man who trusts in the Lord, whose trust is the Lord."*

1 Peter 1:7: *These have come so that the proven genuineness of your faith—of greater worth than gold, which perishes even though refined by fire—may result in praise, glory and honor when Jesus Christ is revealed.*

THOUGHTS TO CONSIDER

Money can be used to purchase goods and services that we need to stay alive, like food, water, and shelter. So when we give away money that could be used to pay for our necessities (or even our wants), we are required to have faith that God will fulfill his promise to provide for our needs (Mt. 6:25–34). Giving up something, whether it is money, possessions, or even our time, is a sacrifice on our part. The main point here is how much are you willing to give to show your faithfulness in God?

**Note to Parents: One mistake that many parents can have a tendency to make is to not allow their children to give when prompted (regardless of the amount a child wants to give). Suppose a child has $100 saved in their piggy bank and at some point your child feels prompted to want to give that money away. Prayerfully consider NOT to stop them. By stopping kids from giving (regardless of the amount), we are hindering their ability to build a reliance on our heavenly father to provide and give them the great joy of giving. Allow your children to give what they are prompted to give.

BIBLE STUDY
Genesis 22

BIBLE STUDY QUESTIONS

1. What did God later do to Abraham?

2. What did God ask Abraham to do?

3. Why would God's request be considered a test of Abraham's faithfulness?

4. How does Abraham's response relate to giving?

5. After reading the story of Abraham and Isaac, what are you willing to give up?

Answers: Page 198

Question 18:

Does our giving reflect Christ in us?

ANSWER:

Yes, giving shows that God's love is in us.

MEMORY VERSE

1 JOHN 3:17

If anyone has material possessions and sees a brother or sister in need but has no pity on them, how can the love of God be in that person?

SCRIPTURE SUPPORT

Proverbs 21:26: *All day long he craves for more, but the righteous give without sparing.*

Matthew 10:8: *"Heal the sick, raise the dead, cleanse those who have leprosy, drive out demons. Freely you have received; freely give."*

Proverbs 18:16: *A gift opens the way and ushers the giver into the presence of the great.*

THOUGHTS TO CONSIDER

The main point is to distinguish 'giving to earn God's love' from 'giving as a reflection of God's love'. Although this could lead to some deep theological debate, the intent here is to emphasize that our giving is a response to what God has given us (salvation from our sin through faith in Jesus Christ). When we understand the magnitude of this gift in our own lives, we respond by reciprocating this act of giving. It is important to note that people can give for many different reasons but, as we talk to others, including our children, our hope is to help them understand that all of our giving is the result of our being made righteous in God's eyes because of our faith and repentance in his Son.

BIBLE STUDY

The question asked could be written to obtain a different, though similar, inquiry: "How is Christ revealed in my giving?" However, before we can truly think biblically about giving, we need to first know Christ as our Lord, our provider, and our counselor. We can do this by repenting of our sin and realizing that only through Christ can we become reconciled to God, our Father. For it is through faith in Christ as our Lord and Savior, and through repentance of our sin, that we become righteous in God's eyes.

This question will not have the Bible Study or Bible Study Questions sections which are replaced with Bible Verses and Prayer to help guide you, your family, and or friends to hear the Word of God in anticipation that the Holy Spirit will help one and all to realize our total depravity and need for a savior.

BIBLE VERSES

Romans 3:23: *for all have sinned and fall short of the glory of God,*

Romans 6:23: *For the wages of sin is death, but the free gift of God is eternal life in Christ Jesus our Lord.*

Romans 5:8: *But God demonstrates His own love toward us, in that while we were yet sinners, Christ died for us.*

John 3:16: *"For God so loved the world, that He gave His only begotten Son, that whoever believes in Him shall not perish, but have eternal life."*

Romans 10:9: *because if thou shalt confess with thy mouth "Jesus as Lord," and shalt believe in thy heart that God raised him from the dead, thou shalt be saved:*

1 John 1:9: *If we confess our sins, He is faithful and righteous to forgive us our sins and to cleanse us from all unrighteousness.*

John 1:12: *But as many as received Him, to them He gave the right to become children of God, even to those who believe in His name:*

Ephesians 2:8–9: *For by grace you have been saved through faith; and that not of yourselves, it is the gift of God; not as a result of works, so that no one may boast.*

2 Corinthians 5:17: *Therefore if anyone is in Christ, he is a new creature; the old things passed away; behold, new things have come.*

Ephesians 1:7: *In Him we have redemption through His blood, the forgiveness of our trespasses, according to the riches of His grace.*

Prayer

Heavenly Father,

May your Word rest upon us as we read these verses. May the act of hearing your words prompt us to acknowledge that we are sinners and have rebelled against your perfect ways. You, and you alone, provide new mercies and grace each day through our new and revitalized faith in your son, Christ Jesus. For as we read, it was by his death and your gift of grace—not by our works—that allows us to be called your children, heirs with Christ, your son.

Lord, we pray that those reciting (and hearing) this prayer accept and acknowledge we are all sinners and have need to repent, to turn away from our sinful nature, and believe in the work and worth of Jesus Christ. Allow the Holy Spirit to lead us each day as we strive to know you more, seek the things of your divine nature, and become a new creature. May this book be used as a tool to continually guide us to repentance and faith in Christ.

Amen.

Question 19:

Why do we give to our neighbor?

ANSWER:

We give to our neighbor to show our true love for them as in Christ.

 MEMORY VERSE

2 Corinthians 8:8

I say this not as a command, but to prove by the earnestness of others that your love also is genuine.

SCRIPTURE SUPPORT

2 Corinthians 9:10–11: *He who supplies seed to the sower and bread for food will supply and multiply your seed for sowing and increase the harvest of your righteousness. You will be enriched in every way to be generous in every way, which through us will produce thanksgiving to God.*

Nehemiah 8:10: *Then he said to them, "Go your way. Eat the fat and drink sweet wine and send portions to anyone who has nothing ready, for this day is holy to our Lord. And do not be grieved, for the joy of the Lord is your strength."*

Deuteronomy 15:10: *You shall give to him freely, and your heart shall not be grudging when you give to him, because for this the Lord your God will bless you in all your work and in all that you undertake.*

THOUGHTS TO CONSIDER

Previously, we identified that our giving is a response to what God has done for us. So how can we take this and apply it to our lives? We can demonstrate that same love to our neighbors. Keep in mind that "neighbors" in this context is not restricted to only those in your neighborhood but, rather, is inclusive of everyone. You see, when we give, we put ourselves in the position to explain why we are giving. It is an opportunity to share the gospel—to demonstrate that we give because God first gave (and continues to give) to us. Giving is one indicator of our love for them, just as when God gave his Son to us is an indicator of his love for us.

BIBLE STUDY
Deuteronomy 15:1–15

BIBLE STUDY QUESTIONS

1. What is the first thing we shouldn't do when seeing a poor brother?

2. What, then, shall we do when seeing a poor brother?

3. How is Deuteronomy 15:9 to be interpreted?

4. What will the Lord do if we give freely and without grudging in our hearts?

5. Why was the practice of cancelling debts every seven years established by God?

6. Why were the Hebrew masters commanded to give liberally from their livestock and storehouses?

7. Why were the Hebrew masters commanded to give liberally from their livestock and storehouses?

Answers: Page 200

Question 20:

What does giving prove to us?

ANSWER:

Our giving proves that Jesus has complete Lordship over our possessions.

 MEMORY VERSE

ISAIAH **40:31**

but those who hope in the Lord will renew their strength they will soar on wings like eagles; they will run and not grow weary, they will walk and not be faint.

SCRIPTURE SUPPORT

Matthew 19:21–22: *Jesus said to him, "If you would be perfect, go, sell what you possess and give to the poor, and you will have treasure in heaven; and come, follow me."*

Luke 18:22–23: *When Jesus heard this, he said to him, "One thing you still lack. Sell all that you have and distribute to the poor, and you will have treasure in heaven; and come, follow me."*

2 Corinthians 9:8: *And God is able to bless you abundantly, so that in all things at all times, having all that you need, you will abound in every good work.*

THOUGHTS TO CONSIDER

Giving is symptomatic of our response to what Jesus Christ has done in our lives and in the realization that *"he gave himself up for us"* (Eph. 5:2). Once we accept Christ as our Lord and Savior, we become stewards of his possessions. As we continue to learn more and grow closer to God, our heart should change from what we want to what God wants. Part of what God wants is for us to be generous, with an overflow of the Fruits of the Spirit (love, joy, peace, patience, kindness, goodness, faithfulness, gentleness, and self-control [Gal. 5:22–23]).

BIBLE STUDY
Read Galatians 5

BIBLE STUDY QUESTIONS

1. How does giving to our neighbor reveal *love* in us?

2. How does giving to our neighbor reveal *joy* in us?

3. How does giving to our neighbor reveal *peace* in us?

4. How does giving to our neighbor reveal *patience* in us?

5. How does giving to our neighbor reveal *kindness* in us?

6. How does giving to our neighbor reveal *goodness* in us?

7. How does giving to our neighbor reveal *faithfulness* in us?

8. How does giving to our neighbor reveal *gentleness* in us?

9. How does giving to our neighbor reveal *self-control* in us?

Answers: Page 202

God's Perspective
on Giving

Question 21:

What is God's attitude toward giving?

ANSWER:

God loves us so much that he gave us the ultimate perfect gift, Jesus Christ.

MEMORY VERSE

JOHN 3:16

"For God so loved the world, that he gave his only Son, that whoever believes in him should not perish but have eternal life."

SCRIPTURE SUPPORT

James 1:17: *Every good gift and every perfect gift is from above, coming down from the Father of lights, with whom there is no variation or shadow due to change.*

Romans 8:32: *He who did not spare His own Son, but delivered Him over for us all, how will He not also with Him free give us all things?*

Acts 8:20: *But Peter said to him, "May your silver perish with you, because you thought you could obtain the gift of God with money!"*

THOUGHTS TO CONSIDER

When we talk about what God has given us and his attitude toward giving, we need to understand that God existed from the beginning; he was not created by anyone or anything. He is the Alpha and Omega, the beginning and the end. Therefore, everything that has been made has been given to us to steward for our use. When we recognize that God made all things and owns all things, then we realize that God continually gives to his creation. This is his very nature: *"For God so loved the world that he gave his one and only Son"* (John 3:16a), a part of the Holy Trinity, to be our mode of salvation from sin and our source of faith and hope for being reconciled with God.

BIBLE STUDY
Genesis 1

BIBLE STUDY QUESTIONS

1. What did God give us on the *first* day?

2. What did God give us on the *second* day?

3. What did God give us on the *third* day?

4. What did God give us on the *fourth* day?

5. What did God give us on the *fifth* day?

6. What did God gives us on the *sixth* day?

7. What was the ultimate gift that God gave to his creation?

Answers: Page 205

Question 22:

What is to be our attitude toward giving?

ANSWER:

We are to be cheerful givers, giving in love.

MEMORY VERSE

2 CORINTHIANS 9:7

Each one must give as he has decided in his heart, not reluctantly or under compulsion, for God loves a cheerful giver.

SCRIPTURE SUPPORT

1 Corinthians 13:3: *If I give away all I have, and if I deliver up my body to be burned, but have not love, I gain nothing.*

Exodus 35:5: *Take from among you a contribution to the Lord. Whoever is of a generous heart, let him bring the Lord's contribution: gold, silver, and bronze;*

2 Corinthians 2:3–4: *Do nothing out of selfish ambition or vain conceit. Rather, in humility value others above yourselves, not looking to your own interests but each of you to the interests of the others.*

THOUGHTS TO CONSIDER

One misconception in the church world regarding money is the idea that tithing is our responsibility in giving. However, this is not the case at all. Several things are to be kept in mind when we give: First, God owns everything. Secondly, God does not need our money. Thirdly, God desires that we give as a representative of Christ, who willingly gave up everything for the benefit of others. This attitude is what pleases God. If we give our financial resources out of obligation, it is meaningless in God's eyes.

We can think about giving using the example of an apology. If someone offers an apology to us and screams the response, saying, "I'm SORRY!!!" in a mean and hateful way, does that mean anything? Probably not. Although an apology was given, it does not appear to be genuine or heartfelt. God wants a sincere expression of our faith in him, nothing less.

BIBLE STUDY
1 Chronicles 29

BIBLE STUDY QUESTIONS

1. What is taking place in this passage?

2. Who is responsible for building the temple?

3. What did David tell the Israelites about what he had done as king?

4. What did David personally provide for building the temple? And, why?

5. What did David ask of those in attendance?

6. In your own words, what was David asking?

Answers: Page 207

Question 23:

What does a good attitude in giving bring?

ANSWER:

A good attitude in giving brings blessings of hope, joy, and community with others.

MEMORY VERSE

DEUTERONOMY 15:10

Give generously to them and do so without a grudging heart; then because of this the Lord your God will bless you in all your work and in everything you put your hand to.

SCRIPTURE SUPPORT

1 Chronicles 29:14–17: *But who am I, and what is my people, that we should be able thus to offer willingly? For all things come from you, and of your own have we given you. For we are strangers before you and sojourners, as all our fathers were. Our days on the earth are like a shadow, and there is no abiding. O Lord our God, all this abundance that we have provided for building you a house for your holy name comes from your hand and is all your own. I know, my God, that you test the heart and have pleasure in uprightness. In the uprightness of my heart I have freely offered all these things, and now I have seen your people, who are present here, offering freely and joyously to you.*

Proverbs 11:24–25: *One gives freely, yet grows all the richer; another withholds what he should give, and only suffers want. Whoever brings blessing will be enriched, and one who waters will himself be watered.*

2 Corinthians 9:6: *The point is this: whoever sows sparingly will also reap sparingly, and whoever sows bountifully will also reap bountifully.*

THOUGHTS TO CONSIDER

God wants us to be cheerful givers. Why does God want this from us? Because God has given us an indescribable sense of joy when we give cheerfully, which is grounded in the knowledge that we give of what God has given to us.

**Note to Parents: Ask your children to think of a time when they had something they were going to give to someone else (like a birthday gift or a Christmas gift). Next, ask them to share about their feelings leading up to giving the gift. For most kids, the excitement is sometimes so high that they cannot contain not giving. This passion is the overflowing joy they have for gift-giving. When this type of feeling is cultivated, our kids can move from a desire to give, to altruistic behavior.

BIBLE STUDY
Romans 15

BIBLE STUDY QUESTIONS

1. What does Paul say is the obligation of the strong?

2. What brings us hope?

3. What is Paul's request? And, how are we to do it?

4. Reflect on Romans 15:13. How does hope, joy, peace in believing, and community relate to our giving?

Answers: Page 210

Question 24:

Can we give with a poor attitude?

ANSWER:

No, our attitude is more important than the amount we give.

MEMORY VERSE

PSALM 139:23–24

Search me, O God, and know my heart! Try me and know my thoughts! And see if there be any grievous way in my, and lead me in the way everlasting.

SCRIPTURE SUPPORT

Matthew 23:23: *Woe to you, scribes and Pharisees, hypocrites! For you tithe mint and dill and cumin, and have neglected the weightier matters of the law: justice and mercy and faithfulness. These you ought to have done, without neglecting the others.*

Philippians 2:14–15: *Do all things without grumbling or questioning, that you may be blameless and innocent, children of God without blemish in the midst of a crooked and twisted generation, among whom you shine as lights in the world,*

James 4:10: *Humble yourselves before the Lord, and he will exalt you.*

THOUGHTS TO CONSIDER

As you may have noticed, the recurring theme throughout this book is the fundamental point that God is the owner of all things and he is more concerned with our heart than with our possessions. This theme is demonstrated throughout the Scriptures and through the overarching narrative of the Bible (God's creation, man's fall, Jesus' redemption, and reconciliation of believers).

The only way to have an appropriate attitude toward giving is to know Christ as our Lord, our provider, our counselor, and the giver of our salvation. We can do this by repenting of our sin and realizing that only through Christ can we be reconciled back to God our Father and become righteous in God's eyes.

This question will not have the Bible Study or Bible Study Questions sections which are replaced with Bible Verses and Prayer to help guide you, your family, and or friends to hear the Word of God in anticipation that the Holy Spirit will help one and all to realize our total depravity and need for a savior.

BIBLE VERSES

Romans 3:23: *for all have sinned and fall short of the glory of God,*

Romans 6:23: *For the wages of sin is death, but the free gift of God is eternal life in Christ Jesus our Lord.*

Romans 5:8: *But God demonstrates His own love toward us, in that while we were yet sinners, Christ died for us.*

John 3:16: *"For God so loved the world, that He gave His only begotten Son, that whoever believes in Him shall not perish, but have eternal life."*

Romans 10:9: *that if you confess with your mouth Jesus as Lord, and believe in your heart that God raised Him from the dead, you will be saved;*

1 John 1:9: *If we confess our sins, He is faithful and righteous to forgive us our sins and to cleanse us from all unrighteousness.*

John 1:12: *But as many as received Him, to them He gave the right to become children of God, even to those who believe in His name,*

Ephesians 2:8–9: *For by grace you have been saved through faith; and that not of yourselves, it is the gift of God; not as a result of works, so that no one may boast.*

2 Corinthians 5:17: *Therefore if anyone is in Christ, he is a new creature; the old things passed away; behold, new things have come.*

Ephesians 1:7: *In Him we have redemption through His blood, the forgiveness of our trespasses, according to the riches of His grace.*

Prayer

Heavenly Father,

May your Word rest upon us as we read these verses. May the act of hearing your words prompt us to acknowledge that we are sinners and have rebelled against your perfect ways. You, and you alone, provide new mercies and grace each day through our new and revitalized faith in your son, Christ Jesus. For as we read, it was by his death and your gift of grace—not by our works—that allows us to be called your children, heirs with Christ, your son.

Lord, we pray that those reciting (and hearing) this prayer accept and acknowledge we are all sinners and have need to repent, to turn away from our sinful nature, and believe in the work and worth of Jesus Christ. Allow the Holy Spirit to lead us each day as we strive to know you more, seek the things of your divine nature, and become a new creature. May this book be used as a tool to continually guide us to repentance and faith in Christ.

Amen.

Attitude of Giving

Question 25:

Should giving become our primary focus?

ANSWER:

No, our primary focus is to ensure all glory is pointed back to Christ.

 MEMORY VERSE

1 PETER 4:11

Whoever speaks, as one who speaks oracles of God; whoever serves, as one who serves by the strength that God supplies—in order that in everything God may be glorified through Jesus Christ. To him belong glory and dominion forever and ever. Amen.

SCRIPTURE SUPPORT

Matthew 26:6–13: *Now when Jesus was at Bethany in the house of Simon the leper, a woman came up to him with an alabaster flask of very expensive ointment, and she poured it on his head as he reclined at table. And when the disciples saw it, they were indignant, saying, "Why this waste? For this could have been sold for a large sum and given to the poor." But Jesus, aware of this, said to them, "Why do you trouble the woman? For she has done a beautiful thing to me. For you always have the poor with you, but you will not always have me. In pouring this ointment on my body, she has done it to prepare me for burial. Truly, I say to you, wherever this gospel is proclaimed in the whole world, what she has done will also be told in memory of her."*

Ecclesiastes 12:13: *The end of the matter; all has been heard. Fear God and keep his commandments, for this is the whole duty of man.*

Isaiah 43:7: *Everyone who is called by my name, whom I created for my glory, who I formed and made.*

THOUGHTS TO CONSIDER

In reference to giving, we need to determine our chief motivation. Do we give our money, resources, and time as a response to our belief in Christ, or do we give with an expectation of self-exaltation? For Christians, we should give because Christ gave his life for us and we desire to emulate his example by sacrificing our time and resources for others. This is in opposition to attempting to gain self-recognition through one's giving. Our giving should glorify God, the ultimate giver, rather than ourselves.

**Note to Parents: This is a concept can be very challenging to grasp. It may be helpful to reflect on whether giving is a cause or an effect. Kids should be able to understand cause and effect, although they may not know what the terms mean. The "cause" is the reason for the "effect." In other words, a cause always comes first and then the effect always comes after the cause.

BIBLE STUDY
1 Chronicles 16 and Acts 13:23

BIBLE STUDY QUESTIONS

1. What event was being celebrated by the Israelites?
2. During this time of celebration, how does David start his speech?
3. What is David asking of the Israelites?
4. What was the focus of the last part of David's song?
5. Why did God select David as king?
6. How does David's story connect to the answer that our primary purpose is to glorify God?

Answers: Page 214

QUESTION 26:

What does God's Word say about our reward for giving?

ANSWER:

We will be blessed and have an increase in heaven.

 MEMORY VERSE

MATTHEW 19:21

Jesus said to him, "If you would be perfect, go, sell what you possess and give to the poor, and you will have treasure in heaven; and come, follow me."

SCRIPTURE SUPPORT

Matthew 6:20: *"But lay up for yourselves treasures in heaven, where neither moth nor rust destroys and where thieves do not break in and steal."*

1 Timothy 6:17–19: *As for the rich in this present age, charge them not to be haughty, nor to set their hopes on the uncertainty of riches, but on God, who richly provides us with everything to enjoy. They are to do good, to be rich in good works, to be generous and ready to share, thus storing up treasure for themselves as a good foundation for the future, so that they may take hold of that which is truly life.*

Acts 20:35: *"In all things I have shown you that by working hard in this way we must help the weak and remember the words of the Lord Jesus, how he himself said, 'It is more blessed to give than to receive.'"*

THOUGHTS TO CONSIDER

The catechism question posed here is about "our reward for giving" which may lead to a misunderstanding of Scripture if not appropriately put in context. For many, when we think that we will have an increase from our giving, we automatically assume that this "increase" is a financial increase and that is not always the case. By giving, we do lay up for ourselves treasures that are in heaven, as Jesus tells us in Matthew 6:20. How wonderful it is to know that we can start investing in our heavenly bank accounts while still here on earth!

BIBLE STUDY
John 14:1–12 and 1 Corinthians 2

BIBLE STUDY QUESTIONS

1. What does Jesus say to his disciples to comfort them?

2. Where is Jesus getting ready to go? And, what will he do next?

3. What did Jesus promise?

4. According to his first letter to Corinth, what did Paul hope our faith would be built upon?

5. How does giving play a part in our heavenly treasure?

Answers: Page 218

Question 27:

What does God say he will do for those who give?

ANSWER:

God can increase our responsibility to steward more of his possessions.

MEMORY VERSE

PROVERBS 3:9–10

Honor the LORD with your wealth and with the firstfruits of all your produce; then your barns will be filled with plenty, and your vats will be bursting with wine.

SCRIPTURE SUPPORT

2 Chronicles 31:10: *Azariah the chief priest, who was of the house of Zadok, answered him, "Since they began to bring the contributions into the house of the Lord, we have eaten and had enough and have plenty left, for the Lord has blessed his people, so that we have this large amount left."*

Proverbs 11:24–25: *One gives freely, yet grows all the richer; another withholds what he should give, and only suffers want. Whoever brings blessing will be enriched, and one who waters will himself be watered.*

Luke 6:38: *"Give, and it will be given to you. Good measure, pressed down, shaken together, running over, will be put into your lap. For with the measure you use it will be measured back to you."*

THOUGHTS TO CONSIDER

When we appropriately manage the responsibility given to us by another, then the natural inclination in the relationship is to be given more responsibility. It is so important to remember that our money and possessions are not our own, but owned by God. God then can give responsibility and take it away as he sees fit. If we manage God's resources in a manner that aligns with the way he intends his possessions be handled, it seems reasonable and in line with God's character that he will then assign greater responsibility to us.

BIBLE STUDY
Luke 12:14-48

BIBLE STUDY QUESTIONS

1. What was Peter's question to Jesus?

2. How did Jesus answer Peter?

3. In the parable of the faithful steward, what did Jesus say happens to the servant who is found to be faithful and a wise manager, as one doing the will of the master?

4. Did Jesus answer Peter's questions?

5. In your own words, what is the meaning of Jesus' parable of the faithful steward?

Answers: Page 220

Question 28:

Does God challenge us to give?

┌─ ANSWER: ──────────────────────

Yes, the only test God seeks for us to challenge
him on is giving.

└────────────────────────────────

 MEMORY VERSE

MALACHI 3:10

*"Bring the full tithe into the storehouse, that there may be
food in my house. And thereby put me to the test," says the
LORD of hosts, "if I will not open the windows of heaven
for you and pour down for you a blessing until there is no
more need."*

SCRIPTURE SUPPORT

1 John 4:1: *Beloved, do not believe every spirit, but test the spirits to see
whether they are from God, for many false prophets have gone out into the world.*

Matthew 4:7: *Jesus said to him, "Again it is written, 'You shall not put the
Lord your God to the test.'"*

Deuteronomy 6:16: *You shall not put the Lord your God to the test, as
you tested him at Massah.*

THOUGHTS TO CONSIDER

Can you imagine if everyone set out to test God by their giving? What if generosity became our matrix of success? What would the world look like? God's very nature is to give, as we have already seen. This "challenge" given by God can be fun to challenge others to try (especially kids). Who can win the generosity game? The results may just surprise you! As you will see in the Bible Study section, when God stirs our hearts to give, we see the "fruit" that it produces.

BIBLE STUDY

Exodus 35; 36:1-7

BIBLE STUDY QUESTIONS

1. Describe what is happening in the setting of Exodus 35?

2. What is one of the conditions Moses set for those who were to bring forth a contribution of gold, silver, bronze, and other supplies for the Tabernacle?

3. After hearing the supplies needed for building the Tabernacle, what influenced those who were to come back with supplies?

4. What type of offering did the children of Israel bring for the Lord?

5. Who were the two individuals tasked with overseeing the building project?

6. Once the craftsmen were given their respective tasks, what concern did they express to Moses?

7. What common theme is found in the following verses: Exodus 35:5, 21, 22, 26, and 39?

8. What is the significance of the identified common theme?

Answers: Page 223

Application of Giving

Question 29:

What is sacrificial giving?

> **ANSWER:**
>
> Sacrificial giving is to give up something that requires a change in our life.

 MEMORY VERSE

2 Corinthians 8:3

For they gave according to their means, as I can testify, and beyond their means, of their own accord,

SCRIPTURE SUPPORT

Mark 12:41–44: *And he sat down opposite the treasury and watched the people putting money into the offering box. Many rich people put in large sums. And a poor widow came and put in two small copper coins, which make a penny. And he called his disciples to him and said to them, "Truly, I say to you, this poor widow has put in more than all those who are contributing to the offering box. For they all contributed out of their abundance, but she out of her poverty has put in everything she had, all she had to live on."*

2 Corinthians 8:1–4: *We want you to know, brothers, about the grace of God that has been given among the churches of Macedonia, for in a severe test of affliction, their abundance of joy and their extreme poverty have overflowed in a wealth of generosity on their part. For they gave according to their means, as I can testify, and beyond their means, of their own accord, begging us earnestly for the favor of taking part in the relief of the saints.*

Acts 4:34: *There was not a needy person among them, for as many as were owners of lands or houses sold them and brought the proceeds of what was sold.*

THOUGHTS TO CONSIDER

Some may argue that there is no real difference between giving and sacrificial giving since, whenever we give something away, we are always sacrificing our use of it. This may be true in one sense, but there is a deeper perspective on sacrificial giving: it requires that we give up something we need—not want. Sacrificial giving is not about bequeathing out of our excess; rather, it is an exhibition of one's faith because such giving creates a deeper dependence on Christ's provision.

BIBLE STUDY
Leviticus 6:1–5 and Luke 19:1–10

BIBLE STUDY QUESTIONS

1. Where does the story about Zacchaeus take place?

2. What do we know about Zacchaeus?

3. What did the crowd think about Jesus going to the home of Zacchaeus?

4. After Zacchaeus met with Jesus, what did he proclaim he would do?

5. Refer to Leviticus 6:1–5. What would Zacchaeus be required to pay according to the Levite law?

6. Would Zacchaeus' giving be considered sacrificial?

Answers: Page 228

Question 30:

Prior to the OT law, what were the Israelites required to give back to the Lord?

ANSWER:

The Israelites were instructed to give three separate tithes: the Levitical tithe, the annual festival tithe, and the tri-annual poor tithe.

 MEMORY VERSE

GENESIS 14:20

And blessed by God Most High, who has delivered your enemies into your hand!" And Abram gave him a tenth of everything.

SCRIPTURE SUPPORT

Deuteronomy 14:22–27: *You shall tithe all the yield of your seed that comes from the field year by year. And before the Lord your God, in the place that he will choose, to make his name dwell there, you shall eat the tithe of your grain, of your wine, and of your oil, and the firstborn of your herd and flock, that you may learn to fear the Lord your God always. And if the way is too long for you, so that you are not able to carry the tithe, when the Lord your God blesses you, because the place is too far from you, which the Lord your God chooses, to set his name there, then you shall turn it into money and bind up* *the money in your hand and go to the place that the Lord your God chooses and spend the money for whatever you desire—oxen or sheep or wine or strong drink, whatever your appetite craves. And you shall eat there before the Lord your God and rejoice, you and your household. And you shall not neglect the Levite who is within your towns, for he has no portion or inheritance with you.*

Deuteronomy 14:28–29: *At the end of every three years you shall bring out all the tithe of your produce in the same year and lay it up within your towns. And the Levite, because he has no portion or inheritance with you, and the sojourner, the fatherless, and the widow, who are within your towns, shall come and eat and be filled, that the Lord your God may bless you in all the work of your hands that you do.*

Leviticus 27:30–32: *"'Every tithe of the land, whether of the seed of the land or of the fruit of the trees, is the LORD's: it is holy to the LORD. If a man wishes to redeem some of his tithe, he shall add a fifth to it. And every tithe of herds and flocks, every tenth animal of all that pass under the herdsman's staff, shall be holy to the LORD.'"*

THOUGHTS TO CONSIDER

The concept of tithing (or giving a tenth) is very common in the Christian faith when, as it relates to giving. The Israelites in the Old Testament were ordered to tithe as a means to support the Levites, since they received no inheritance from the Lord. The tithe was used to ensure they had sufficient food for God's house (Storehouse). The Israelites were also required to bring a tithe for the annual festival to celebrate the blessings of our Lord. Finally, every three years, they were required to give to the poor. When we look at all these requirements and, depending on how they actually calculated the base amount for their tithe, the Israelites paid roughly 21–27% of their possessions to the Lord.

BIBLE STUDY
Numbers 18

BIBLE STUDY QUESTIONS

1. What did the Lord tell Aaron that he and his son's would bear from the Lord's people?

2. What was the responsibility of the tribe of Levi?

3. What did the Lord give Aaron and the tribe Levi charge over?

4. Which offerings were the Levi tribe given?

5. Was there anything else the Levi tribe was given?

6. What was the inheritance supposed to be for the tribe of Levi?

7. In addition to the offerings, what else did the Lord give to the Levites?

8. Were there any conditions the Levites needed to follow related to the tithe?

Answers: Page 230

Question 31:

Are we to give sacrificially?

ANSWER:

Yes, we should be willing to give up something we need to others. Giving should cost us something.

MEMORY VERSE

2 Corinthians 8:1–2

We want you to know, brothers, about the grace of God that has been given among the churches of Macedonia, for in a severe test of affliction, their abundance of joy and their extreme poverty have overflowed in a wealth of generosity on their part.

SCRIPTURE SUPPORT

2 Samuel 24:21–24: *And Araunah said, "Why has my lord the king come to his servant?" David said, "To buy the threshing floor from you, in order to build an altar to the Lord, that the plague may be averted from the people." Then Araunah said to David, "Let my lord the king take and offer up what seems good to him. Here are the oxen for the burnt offering and the threshing sledges and the yokes of the oxen for the wood. All this, O king, Araunah gives to the king." And Araunah said to the king, "May the Lord your God accept you." But the king said to Araunah, "No, but I will buy it from you for a price. I will not offer burnt offerings to the Lord my God that cost me nothing." So David bought the threshing floor and the oxen for fifty shekels of silver.*

1 Chronicles 21:22–24: *And David said to Ornan, "Give me the site of the threshing floor that I may build on it an altar to the LORD—give it to me at its full price—that the plague may be averted from the people." Then Ornan said to David, "Take it, and let my lord the king do what seems good to him. See, I give the oxen for burnt offerings and the threshing sledges for the wood and the wheat for a grain offering; I give it all." But King David said to Ornan, "No, but I will buy them for the full price. I will not take for the LORD what is yours, nor offer burnt offerings that cost me nothing."*

Proverbs 21:26: *All day long he craves for me, but the righteous give without sparing.*

THOUGHTS TO CONSIDER

As Christians, we are called to give up our life, a complete and utter surrender of sacrifice to Christ, as Christ first gave up his life for us. Unfortunately, in our culture, this idea of sacrificing our lives for Christ has been minimalized. We should have every desire to give up everything that "God owns" (since we do not own anything) for God's glory. Before this makes any sense, though, we must know and believe in what Christ did on our behalf so that we are empowered by the Holy Spirit to emulate him.

This question will not have the Bible Study or Bible Study Questions sections which are replaced with Bible Verses and Prayer to help guide you, your family, and or friends to hear the Word of God in anticipation that the Holy Spirit will help one and all to realize our total depravity and need for a savior.

Read through the Scriptures below, and reflect on Christ's perfect nature in heaven. Consider his willingness to leave his heavenly throne, to be born in the lowest of places, to be the earthly son of a carpenter, and die the death of the worst of criminals. What sacrifice and love Christ exhibits!

BIBLE VERSES

Romans 3:23: *for all have sinned and fall short of the glory of God,*

Romans 6:23: *For the wages of sin is death, but the free gift of God is eternal life in Christ Jesus our Lord.*

Romans 5:8: *But God demonstrates His own love toward us, in that while we were yet sinners, Christ died for us.*

John 3:16: *"For God so loved the world, that He gave His only begotten Son, that whoever believes in Him shall not perish, but have eternal life."*

Romans 10:9: *that if you confess with your mouth Jesus as Lord, and believe in your heart that God raised Him from the dead, you will be saved;*

1 John 1:9: *If we confess our sins, He is faithful and righteous to forgive us our sins and to cleanse us from all unrighteousness.*

John 1:12: *But as many as received Him, to them He gave the right to become children of God, even to those who believe in His name,*

Ephesians 2:8–9: *For by grace you have been saved through faith; and that not of yourselves, it is the gift of God; not as a result of works, so that no one may boast.*

2 Corinthians 5:17: *Therefore if anyone is in Christ, he is a new creature; the old things passed away; behold, new things have come.*

Ephesians 1:7: *In Him we have redemption through His blood, the forgiveness of our trespasses, according to the riches of His grace.*

Prayer

Heavenly Father,

May your Word rest upon us as we read these verses. May the act of hearing your words prompt us to acknowledge that we are sinners and have rebelled against your perfect ways. You, and you alone, provide new mercies and grace each day through our new and revitalized faith in your son, Christ Jesus. For as we read, it was by his death and your gift of grace—not by our works—that allows us to be called your children, heirs with Christ, your son.

Lord, we pray that those reciting (and hearing) this prayer accept and acknowledge we are all sinners and have need to repent, to turn away from our sinful nature, and believe in the work and worth of Jesus Christ. Allow the Holy Spirit to lead us each day as we strive to know you more, seek the things of your divine nature, and become a new creature. May this book be used as a tool to continually guide us to repentance and faith in Christ.

Amen.

Question 32:

What is to be our first financial priority?

> **ANSWER:**
>
> Giving is to be our first financial priority.

MEMORY VERSE

1 CORINTHIANS 16:2

On the first day of every week, each of you is to put something aside and store it up, as he may prosper, so that there will be no collecting when I come.

SCRIPTURE SUPPORT

Exodus 23:10–11: *"For six years you shall sow your land and gather in its yield, but the seventh year you shall let it rest and lie fallow, that the poor of your people may eat; and what they leave the beasts of the field may eat. You shall do likewise with your vineyard, and with your olive orchard."*

Numbers 28:26: *"On the day of the firstfruits, when you offer a grain offering of new grain to the LORD at your Feast of Weeks, you shall have a holy convocation. You shall not do any ordinary work..."*

Proverbs 3:9: *Honor the LORD with your wealth and with the firstfruits of all your produce;*

THOUGHTS TO CONSIDER

If we are not careful, money can create a power hold on our lives. We can quickly begin to think and act as if the money God has allowed us to use is ours. When are we most likely to be tempted to think that what God has given to us is ours? Each time we are given more resources (i.e., our paychecks). When we are blessed with our paychecks, we need to re-establish ourselves to an appropriate relationship with that money. The process of giving a portion of money each time we receive it is one behavior that can keep us in the right frame of mind as we seek to manage the rest of the money as a steward.

BIBLE STUDY
1 Corinthians 16:1–4

BIBLE STUDY QUESTIONS

1. Why do you think Paul starts 1 Corinthians 16:1 with "Now concerning?"

2. What was Paul addressing in the early part of his letter to the Corinthians?

3. How often did Paul suggest the church in Corinth put aside money that was to be given?

4. Why do you think Paul declared the first day of each week as the time to set aside their tithe?

5. How much were the Corinthians supposed to set aside?

Answers: Page 233

Question 33:

Is there a pattern of giving we should follow?

> **ANSWER:**
>
> Yes, we are to give regularly through the prompting from the Holy Spirit.

 MEMORY VERSE

DEUTERONOMY 16:17:

Every man shall give as he is able, according to the blessing of the LORD your God that he has given you.

SCRIPTURE SUPPORT

2 Corinthians 9:7: *Each one must give as he has decided in his heart, not reluctantly or under compulsion, for God loves a cheerful giver.*

1 Corinthians 16:2: *On the first day of every week, each of you is to put something aside and store it up, as he may prosper, so that there will be no collecting when I come.*

Acts 11:29: *So the disciples determined, every one according to his ability, to send relief to the brothers living in Judea.*

THOUGHTS TO CONSIDER

God gives us many patterns in life that we are to follow. One such pattern is that our giving should be done regularly. This was originally established in the Old Testament through the tithe process: the Israelites were to provide for the Temple and the Levitical priesthood. This act was carried over through the writings of Paul to the Corinthians (and the Galatians) as they were instructed to set aside money on a regular basis so that when the money was needed, everyone had it ready to give. If people did not put money aside regularly, then a collection would be needed to support the saints. It is important to know that when we do something regularly, it becomes easier to do.

BIBLE STUDY
Luke 22:14-23

BIBLE STUDY QUESTIONS

1. What is taking place in the Luke 22 passage?

2. What did Jesus partake of first and then pass around to his disciples?

3. What did Jesus partake of second and then pass around to his disciples?

4. What did Jesus say to his disciples after breaking the bread?

5. Why did Jesus command his disciples to take part in the remembrance of the Lord's Supper?

Answers: Page 235

Question 34:

Who should we give to?

> **ANSWER:**
>
> We should give to our local church, missionaries, those who ask of us, the poor, and our enemies.

 MEMORY VERSE

GALATIANS 6:10

So then, as we have opportunity, let us do good to everyone, and especially to those who are of the household of faith.

SCRIPTURE SUPPORT

1 Timothy 5:17–18: *Let the elders who rule well be considered worthy of double honor, especially those who labor in preaching and teaching. For the Scripture says, "You shall not muzzle an ox when it treads out the grain," and, "The laborer deserves his wages."*

Matthew 5:42: *"Give to the one who begs from you, and do not refuse the one who would borrow from you."*

Proverbs 25:21–22: *If your enemy is hungry, give him bread to eat, and if he is thirsty, give him water to drink, for you will heap burning coals on his head, and the Lord will reward you.*

THOUGHTS TO CONSIDER

The answer to this question should be rather simple. You should be willing to give to anyone. Recall that nothing we have belongs to us since we are stewards of what God has given us. Therefore, we must act in a manner pleasing to God. Since we know God gave his only Son (John 3:16), and Jesus gave his life as God (1 Tim. 2:5–6), we can know that we are to be willing to give everything as well (Luke 14:33). Our entire existence revolves around glorifying God (1 Cor. 10:31), being like Christ (1 John 2:6), and demonstrating God's love (1 Cor. 13). These three things come together in our ability to give wherever there is a need.

BIBLE STUDY

Acts 4

BIBLE STUDY QUESTIONS

1. In general, what is taking place at the beginning of Acts 4?

2. What did the Priests and Sadducees do as a result of the actions of Peter and John?

3. According to the reading, how many heard and believed the proclamations of Peter and John?

4. When Peter and John were on trial the next day, what did the people see in them?

5. Peter and John were released on what condition? Did they agree?

6. Peter and John went back to their fellow believers and prayed for continued boldness. What happened next?

7. What was the first revelation that occurred after the Holy Spirit filled everyone?

8. What did the people do as a result of the first revelation? And what did it accomplish?

Answers: Page 236

Question 35:

Do we need to be cautious in our giving?

ANSWER:

Yes, because there will come false teachers
seeking earthly gain.

 MEMORY VERSE

MATTHEW 7:15

*"Beware of false prophets, who come to you in sheep's
clothing but inwardly are ravenous wolves."*

SCRIPTURE SUPPORT

2 Corinthians 2:17: *For we are not, like so many, peddlers of God's word,
but as men of sincerity, as commissioned by God, in the sight of God we speak
in Christ.*

Titus 1:10–11: *For there are many who are insubordinate, empty talkers
and deceivers, especially those of the circumcision party. They must be silenced,
since they are upsetting whole families by teaching for shameful gain what they
ought not to teach.*

2 Peter 2:1–3: *But false prophets also arose among the people, just as there will
be false teachers among you, who will secretly bring in destructive heresies, even
denying the Master who brought them, bringing upon themselves swift destruction.
And many will follow their sensuality and because of them the way of truth will
be blasphemed. And in their greed they will exploit you with false words. Their
condemnation from long ago is not idle, and their destruction is not asleep.*

THOUGHTS TO CONSIDER

Although we can never know the purity of one's motives, as Christians we need to be diligent in where God's resources are going. Again, we are stewards of God's resources and it is our responsibility to manage those resources appropriately in a way that gives God all the glory. As made known in the supporting verses, we are warned that there will be false prophets seeking to profit and take advantage of those inclined to give with little due diligence. It is so very important to continually seek the guidance of the Holy Spirit when it comes to giving, both for promptings to give when there is a need and to protect us from frivolous giving that may not be God honoring.

BIBLE STUDY
Romans 16:17–20

BIBLE STUDY QUESTIONS

1. This section of Scripture is wrapping up one of Paul's most famous letters. What does Paul appeal to the brothers to do?

2. What does Paul say that individuals causing divisions and occasions for stumbling are doing and not doing?

3. Of those who are causing divisions, how are they doing it?

4. Although Paul is optimistic regarding the obedience of his audience, what is his desire for them?

5. Based on Romans 16:20, who is ultimately responsible for the divisions and occasions for stumbling?

Answers: Page 239

Question 36:

What are the benefits of giving to others?

> **ANSWER:**
>
> God will provide for our needs, answer our prayers, give us honor, and bless our work.

 MEMORY VERSE

PROVERBS 19:17

Whoever is generous to the poor lends to the Lord, and he will repay him for his deed.

SCRIPTURE SUPPORT

Proverbs 28:27: *Whoever gives to the poor will not want, but he who hides his eyes will get many a curse.*

Psalm 41:1–3: *Blessed is the one who considers the poor! In the day of trouble the Lord delivers him; the Lord protects him and keeps him alive; he is called blessed in the land; you do not give him up to the will of his enemies. The Lord sustains him on his sickbed; in his illness you restore him to full health.*

Deuteronomy 15:10: *You shall give to him freely, and your heart shall not be grudging when you give to him, because for this the Lord your God will bless you in all your work and in all that you undertake.*

THOUGHTS TO CONSIDER

By now, we should have a good understanding of God's love. Because of his love for us, he desires so much that we become more like the image of Christ, the perfect symbol of one who can demonstrate pure generosity.

In his Word, God has promised that when we give to others, we will receive everything to meet *our needs*, he will listen to our prayers, give honor, and bless our work. These are wonderful benefits. It is important to note, however, that one important benefit is not listed. We do not find in Scripture that God will bless our giving with more money. In other words, we should not think that giving is something we do in order to receive more. Although God may provide us with more of his resources to manage, *it should not be expected*.

BIBLE STUDY
Colossians 1:21–22 and 1 Peter 2:24–25; 4:13

BIBLE STUDY QUESTIONS

1. In 1 Peter 2:24, who is Peter talking about suffering?

2. According to Peter, what did Christ give up for us?

3. What does Peter say was the purpose of Christ's death?

4. According to Paul, what was our state of being before Christ gave us salvation?

5. How were we reconciled back to God?

6. What did Jesus ultimately give us that satisfies all our needs?

Answers: Page 240

Budgeting

Question 37:

What is the biblical purpose of a budget?

 MEMORY VERSE

PROVERBS 27:23–24

Know well the condition of your flocks, and give attention to your herds, for riches do not last forever; and does a crown endure to all generations?

SCRIPTURE SUPPORT

Romans 14:12: *So then each of us will give an account of himself to God.*

Luke 14:28: *"For which of you, desiring to build a tower, does not first sit down and count the cost, whether he has enough to complete it?"*

Ecclesiastes 11:2: *Give a portion to seven, or even to eight, for you know not what disaster may happen on earth.*

THOUGHTS TO CONSIDER

Now that we have a solid understanding of stewardship and recognize that we are merely managers of God's resources, it is important to introduce the concept of a budget. A budget is simply a way to allocate money to future expenses. The process can range in sophistication from a very simple pen and paper budget to an excel spreadsheet or budgeting app. The most important concept of a budget is that we identify—in advance—where money will be spent and how much will be spent on various expenses. As a steward of God's resources, a budget is a tool that helps us keep an account of what God provides us (our income) and where we are spending to give God the most glory (our expenses.)

**Note to Parents: For those with small children, you can define what a budget is. A *budget* is a way that we set a certain amount of money aside for certain payments we have now and will have in the future. This definition can be expanded if you have children that can understand the concepts of having regular and unexpected future payments and knowing that you have a certain amount of money in which to make these payments (your income).

BIBLE STUDY
Luke 14:26-32

BIBLE STUDY QUESTIONS

1. What is the heading in your Bible for the Luke 14:26–32 passage, if one is available?

2. Why do you think Jesus starts talking to the crowds about hating their own family members?

3. Besides "hating" one's family, what else must we do to be a follower of Christ?

4. When sharing the parable about the concept of knowing the cost, what example does Jesus use?

5. What is Jesus implying when referring to "counting the cost?"

6. What is the outcome if we are unable to complete our task due to a lack of planning?

7. What other example of counting cost did Jesus share?

8. How does Jesus finish this set of parables?

Answers: Page 242

Question 38:

What does budgeting our finances do for us?

ANSWER:

Budgeting our finances helps us to prosper by creating order for what God has given to us.

MEMORY VERSE

1 CORINTHIANS 14:40

But all things should be done decently and in order.

SCRIPTURE SUPPORT

1 Corinthians 14:33: *For God is not a God of confusion but of peace. As in all the churches of the saints,*

Proverbs 24:3–4: *By wisdom a house is built, and by understanding it is established; by knowledge the rooms are filled with all precious and pleasant riches.*

Proverbs 21:5: *The plans of the diligent lead surely to abundance, but everyone who is hasty comes only to poverty.*

THOUGHTS TO CONSIDER

It is important to note that God is a god of order. He has created all things to align to his perfect way. Managing money is no different and it is something we should learn at a very early age. When we create a budget, we are putting God's financial resources in an orderly fashion which minimizes confusion about money. We will see a wide variety of examples of the way God has set order in his creation in the Bible Study section. Although the chapters do not speak specifically to money; importantly, they help us to better understand the character of our Lord and Savior.

BIBLE STUDY
Job 38-41

BIBLE STUDY QUESTIONS

1. What does God claim Job is doing? Why is what Job is doing inappropriate?

2. Provide the verses to each activity God does that includes order.

3. After reading these few chapters of God's response to Job, how do you feel about the way God wants us to handle his resources?

Answers: Page 243

Question 39:

How do we get started when creating a budget?

ANSWER:

We are to start by seeking biblically-wise counsel.

 MEMORY VERSE

PROVERBS 20:18

Plans are established by counsel; by wise guidance wage war.

SCRIPTURE SUPPORT

Proverbs 12:15: *The way of a fool is right in his own eyes, but a wise man listens to advice.*

2 Timothy 3:16: *All Scripture is breathed out by God and profitable for teaching, for reproof, for correction, and for training in righteousness,*

Proverbs 21:5: *The plans of the diligent lead surely to abundance, but everyone who is hasty comes only to poverty.*

THOUGHTS TO CONSIDER

If God owns everything, then we need to know what God wants us to do with his resources. Fortunately, we have multiple resources available to direct us when we create a budget. First, God gives us his Word, which we need to be reading every day. Next, God gives us the Holy Spirit to guide us in our thoughts and actions. Thirdly, and the most tangible, we have godly men and women in our lives. We can learn so much from the lives of others, both their success and their failure or regrets. As we begin to be responsible for managing money, take time to seek out individuals in your life and ask them about managing money. Talk to people of all ages in your church, and learn from their wisdom.

 BIBLE STUDY

This question does not have a Bible Study; rather, there is an exercise. Refer to the Interview Guide in Appendix A of this book to start your discussion. Use the Bible Study Questions below to reflect on what you learned.

*Interview your Pastor using the Interview Guide (Appendix A).

BIBLE STUDY QUESTIONS

1. What were your first thoughts as you finished the interview with your pastor?

2. Did any part of the conversation make you feel uncomfortable? If so, explain.

3. Based on what you have learned, how has your view of money changed, if any?

4. How has what you learned influenced the way you plan to manage money in the future?

Saving Money

Question 40:

Does saving money go against Scripture?

> **ANSWER:**
>
> No, but our savings should not be what we depend on?

 MEMORY VERSE

PSALM 62:10

Put no trust in extortion; set no vain hopes on robbery; if riches increase, set not your heart on them.

SCRIPTURE SUPPORT

Timothy 6:17–19: *Command those who are rich in this present world not to be arrogant nor to put their hope in wealth, which is so uncertain, but to put their hope in God, who richly provides us with everything for our enjoyment. Command them to do good, to be rich in good deeds, and to be generous and willing to share. In this way they will lay up treasure for themselves as a firm foundation for the coming age, so that they may take hold of the life that is truly life.*

Mark 6:8: *These were his instructions: "Take nothing for the journey except a staff—no bread, no bag, no money in your belts."*

Luke 5:11: *And when they had brought their boats to land, they left everything and followed him.*

THOUGHTS TO CONSIDER

Are we supposed to give away or spend every last penny the Lord provides us to be faithful? Absolutely not. God provides us resources in order to sustain ourselves and prepare for the unexpected. As you read through the Bible Study section, pay close attention to the common theme.

BIBLE STUDY

Matthew 24:42-43; Luke 12:35-38, 21:36; 1 Corinthians 16:13; Colossians 4:2; and 1 Thessalonians 5:6

BIBLE STUDY QUESTIONS

1. What do all of the Bible Study passages have in common?

2. What do the Bible Study passages teach us about saving?

3. In Luke's gospel, how does saving money help us to "be ready?"

4. In both 1 Corinthians and Colossians, we see God's Word proclaim to be on guard or watchful. How does saving money apply to being watchful or on guard?

Answers: Page 253

Question 41:

What do we need to be cautious about when saving?

ANSWER:

We need not be in a hurry to build wealth nor have wealth as our ultimate goal.

 MEMORY VERSE

PROVERBS 28:20

A faithful man will abound with blessings, but whoever hastens to be rich will not go unpunished.

SCRIPTURE SUPPORT

Proverbs 21:5: *The plans of the diligent lead surely to abundance, but everyone who is hasty comes only to poverty.*

1 Timothy 6:9–11: *But those who desire to be rich fall into temptation, into a snare, into many senseless and harmful desires that plunge people into ruin and destruction. For the love of money is a root of all kinds of evils. It is through this craving that some have wandered away from the faith and pierced themselves with many pangs. But as for you, O man of God, flee these things. Pursue righteousness, godliness, faith, love, steadfastness, gentleness.*

Matthew 6:24: *"No one can serve two masters, for either he will hate the one and love the other, or he will be devoted to the one and despise the other. You cannot serve God and money."*

THOUGHTS TO CONSIDER

Saving is a very important aspect of managing God's resources. We need to save for expected expenses as well as for upcoming known purchases. Unfortunately, saving to quickly build wealth (or for the mere reason of becoming wealthy) can be detrimental. Our Scripture Support verses point to the fact that those who seek wealth quickly end up with little. It is so important to remember that God is our ultimate provider and all our saving is futile without God who provides everything we need.

BIBLE STUDY
Daniel 4

BIBLE STUDY QUESTIONS

1. Who penned Daniel 4?

2. Why is the author writing the letter?

3. What was the setting at the start of the letter?

4. Describe in detail what took place.

5. What was the interpretation of the dream?

6. What does Daniel request of Nebuchadnezzar?

7. What happened in 12 months and then immediately thereafter?

8. What did Nebuchadnezzar do that put him back in his place and how does this apply to our being cautious about striving for wealth?

Answers: Page 255

Wealth Accumulation

Question 42:

Once we have savings, how are we to invest?

ANSWER:

We are to seek the guidance of the Lord and spread out our funds over multiple investments.

 MEMORY VERSE

Ecclesiastes 11:2

Give a portion to seven, or even to eight, for you know not what disaster may happen on earth.

SCRIPTURE SUPPORT

Isaiah 48:17: *Thus says the Lord, your Redeemer, the Holy One of Israel: "I am the Lord your God, who teaches you to profit, who leads you in the way you should go."*

Psalm 32:8: *I will instruct you and teach you in the way you should go; I will counsel you with my eye upon you.*

James 1:5–6: *If any of you lacks wisdom, let him ask God, who gives generously to all without reproach, and it will be given him. But let him ask in faith, with no doubting, for the one who doubts is like a wave of the sea that is driven and tossed by the wind.*

THOUGHTS TO CONSIDER

One of the fundamentals of investing is to grow our money while being mindful not to lose what we have saved. We are able to earn money through our work, take a portion of our earnings and put it aside for savings, and then we can use that saved money to invest. This process can take some time, so we don't want to use investments in a way that would cause us to take on too much risk or loss exposure.

BIBLE STUDY
Matthew 25:14-30

BIBLE STUDY QUESTIONS

1. Who are the characters in the parable of the talents taught by Jesus?

2. In total, how many talents did the master have?

3. What percentage of his property did the master give to each servant?

4. What is the reason the master gave his property to three different people?

Answers: Page 259

Question 43:

Are we to boast about our investment returns?

ANSWER:

No, we are not to boast in our riches.

 MEMORY VERSE

JEREMIAH 9:23–24

Thus says the Lord: "Let not the wise man boast in his wisdom, let not the mighty man boast in his might, let not the rich man boast in his riches, but let him who boasts boast in this, that he understands and knows me, that I am the Lord who practices steadfast love, justice, and righteousness in the earth. For in these things I delight, declares the Lord."

SCRIPTURE SUPPORT

1 Timothy 6:17: *As for the rich in this present age, charge them not to be haughty, nor to set their hopes on the uncertainty of riches, but on God, who richly provides us with everything to enjoy.*

James 1:9–11: *Let the lowly brother boast in his exaltation, and the rich in his humiliation, because like a flower of the grass he will pass away. For the sun rises with its scorching heat and withers the grass; its flower falls, and its beauty perishes. So also will the rich man fade away in the midst of his pursuits.*

James 4:16: *As it is, you boast in your arrogance. All such boasting is evil.*

THOUGHTS TO CONSIDER

To boast is to brag or talk with excessive pride about something. The boasting could be about anything: our ability, our possessions, our family, anything! As can be seen in the Scripture Support verses, God's Word has specific instructions: we are not to not to boast about our wealth. Why are we not to boast? Primarily because the money is not ours; it is all God's. Remember that we are stewards—what we possess by God's grace is not ours.

BIBLE STUDY
Philippians 3:1–8

BIBLE STUDY QUESTIONS

1. What does Paul warn us not to put our confidence in?

2. What are the reasons Paul has for putting confidence in the flesh?

3. After Paul's conversion, how did he view all these things that he could "boast" in as a Jew?

4. What then should we be confident in; in other words, what are we able to boast about?

Answers: Page 261

Question 44:

Can we trust in our savings and investments?

ANSWER:

No, we are not to set our dependence on our wealth.

 MEMORY VERSE

1 TIMOTHY 6:17

As for the rich in this present age, charge them not to be haughty, nor to set their hopes on the uncertainty of riches, but on God, who richly provides us with everything to enjoy.

SCRIPTURE SUPPORT

Jeremiah 49:4–5: *"Why do you boast of your valleys, O faithless daughter, who trusted in her treasures, saying, 'Who will come against me?' Behold, I will bring terror upon you, declares the Lord God of hosts, from all who are around you and you shall be driven out, every man straight before him, with none to gather the fugitives."*

Jeremiah 48:7: *"For, because you trusted in your works and your treasures, you also shall be taken; and Chemosh shall go into exile with his priests and his officials."*

John 15:5: *"I am the vine; you are the branches. Whoever abides in me and I in him, he it is that bears much fruit, for apart from me you can do nothing."*

THOUGHTS TO CONSIDER

This question about whether we are to trust in our savings and investments is probably one of the most challenging as it relates to applying financial discipleship to our life. As our wealth increases, it is our nature to turn our trust and dependence on this wealth to sustain us, and it is extremely easy to lose our dependence on Christ, who is our Lord and Savior. There is a natural tendency to "not bother God" when we have the resources to accomplish what we want or acquire something (to pay for goods or services when we have the money available). In circumstances like these, what we miss is the fact that God desires to be in our everyday lives, not just when our resources are scarce.

BIBLE STUDY

2 Chronicles 14–16

BIBLE STUDY QUESTIONS

1. After 10 years of Asa's reign, who came out to start a war with Judah?
2. What was Asa's first response when he went out to meet Zerah's army?
3. What was the outcome of the battle?
4. In 2 Chronicles 15, what did Azariah tell Asa?
5. What event occurred in the 36th year of Asa's reign?
6. What did Asa do in response to the building of Ramah?
7. Did Asa's strategy work? Explain.
8. What happened in response to Asa placing trust in the covenant made with Ben-hadad instead of Jehovah?
9. Why do you think that Asa did not seek God in the second crisis?

Answers: Page 262

Question 45:

What are we to do with the wealth we create from our investments?

ANSWER:

We are instructed to use wealth to provide for our family and to give generously.

 MEMORY VERSE

1 JOHN 3:17–18

But if anyone has the world's goods and sees his brother in need, yet closes his heart against him, how does God's love abide in him? Little children, let us not love in word or talk but in deed and in truth.

SCRIPTURE SUPPORT

1 Timothy 6:18: *They are to do good, to be rich in good works, to be generous and ready to share,*

1 Timothy 5:8: *But if anyone does not provide for his relatives, and especially for members of his household, he has denied the faith and is worse than an unbeliever.*

Matthew 6:19–21: *"Do not lay up for yourselves treasures on earth, where moth and rust destroy and where thieves break in and steal, but lay up for yourselves treasures in heaven, where neither moth nor rust destroys and where thieves do not break in and steal. For where your treasure is, there your heart will be also."*

THOUGHTS TO CONSIDER

Material possessions have two purposes: 1) to provide for our families, and 2) to give away. The challenge with this response is that "providing" for our families is such a vague answer. How much do we need to provide for our family? This question is best answered through consistent prayer and seeking wise counsel. What is most important is that these two purposes are not mutually exclusive. In other words, we need to provide for our families, and we need to give (share). How each of these are divided is determined through our prayer life, but both are to be evident in our lives.

BIBLE STUDY
Numbers 18:8–32 and Deuteronomy 14:22–29

BIBLE STUDY QUESTIONS

1. According to Numbers 18, what were the Israelites commanded to support?

2. What were the Israelites to support with their resources, according to Deuteronomy 14:22–27?

3. How often were the two offerings required?

4. Review Deuteronomy 14:28–29. What were the Israelites supposed to support and how often?

5. How much was each of the three offerings supposed to be?

6. What were the Israelites to do with the remaining portion of their resources?

Answers: Page 267

Borrowing and Lending

Question 46:

What expectations should we have when we lend to someone?

┌─ ANSWER: ─────────────────────────────────┐

We should not expect anything in return.

└──┘

 MEMORY VERSE

LUKE 6:34–35

"And if you lend to those from whom you expect to receive, what credit is that to you? Even sinners lend to sinners, to get back the same amount. But love your enemies, and do good, and lend, expecting nothing in return, and your reward will be great, and you will be sons of the Most High, for he is kind to the ungrateful and the evil."

SCRIPTURE SUPPORT

Ezekiel 18:7, 9, 16–17: *Does not oppress anyone, but restores to the debtor his pledge, commits no robbery, gives his bread to the hungry and covers the naked with a garment,... walks in my statutes, and keeps my rules by acting faithfully—he is righteous; he shall surely live, declares the Lord God....does not oppress anyone, exacts no pledge, commits no robbery, but gives his bread to the hungry and covers the naked with a garment, withholds his hand from iniquity, takes no interest or profit, obeys my rules, and walks in my statutes; he shall not die for his father's iniquity; he shall surely live.*

Proverbs 19:17: *Whoever is generous to the poor lends to the Lord, and he will repay him for his deed.*

Matthew 5:42: *"Give to the one who begs from you, and do not refuse the one who would borrow from you."*

THOUGHTS TO CONSIDER

It may be challenging to accept that when we lend money to some-one, we need to think of this "loan" as a gift and have no expecta-tions that it will be repaid. In the Memory Verse from Luke's gospel, the words of Jesus proclaim that we are to be better than "sinners" who lend and expect to get back the same amount. As Christians, we are to do good and lend to others but then have no expectation of getting the money back. In the eyes of Christ, lending to another and giving to another are the same thing!

BIBLE STUDY
Deuteronomy 15:1–11

BIBLE STUDY QUESTIONS

1. What were the Israelites supposed to do every seven years with other Israelites who owed them money?

2. How were the Israelites to handle the poor among them?

3. What did Moses caution the Israelites about con-cerning the 7th year debt cancellation?

4. According to Moses, what was to be the Israelites' attitude toward giving?

5. How does our attitude toward giving relate to not expecting anything in return when we lend to others?

Answers: Page 271

Question 47:

Is it okay to borrow money?

ANSWER:

Borrowing money is not a sin, but it should be done with prayerful consideration.

 MEMORY VERSE

PROVERBS 22:7

The rich rules over the poor and the borrower is the slave to the lender.

SCRIPTURE SUPPORT

Luke 6:30: *"Give to everyone who begs from you, and from ne who takes away your good do not demand them back."*

Exodus 22:14: *"If a man borrows anything of his neighbor, and it is injured or dies, the owner not being with it, he shall make full restitution."*

Luke 16:11: *"If then you have not been faithful in the unrighteous wealth, who will entrust to you the true riches."*

THOUGHTS TO CONSIDER

Inside the church, the word *debt* almost seems like a bad word, for some even a sin. Debt, or the act of borrowing money, is never referenced in the Bible as sin and is actually part of the Law outlined in Deuteronomy. As we think about borrowing money, two fundamental questions need to be asked: *"As a steward of God's resources, is borrowing money for (fill in the purpose here) giving God the glory he deserves? And, "Have I spent time in prayer over this borrowing decision?"* As will be seen in the Bible Study section, we need to be very cautious about our motivations, specifically about borrowing money. *Borrowing*, by its very nature, means acquiring something (typically, money, but it doesn't have to be) and paying a fee (i.e., interest) for its use. Then, at some point in the future, we are required to repay the initial borrowing (principal), plus the interest. It is not the process of borrowing that is the issue, but the reason behind *why* we are borrowing.

BIBLE STUDY
Haggai 1–2

BIBLE STUDY QUESTIONS

1. What was the first thing that the prophet Haggai told to Zerubbabel and Joshua?

2. What question did Haggai then pose to the people of Israel?

3. What were the outcomes of the Israelites' focus on themselves?

4. What should the Israelites have focused on instead of their own possessions?

5. What did the Lord declare through Haggai once the people accepted his message?

6. How many times does the word "consider" occur in the book of Haggai?

7. What is the reason for such a strong emphasis?

Answers: Page 273

Question 48:

What are our responsibilities if we borrow money?

ANSWER:

We are to repay everything owed.

 MEMORY VERSE

PSALM 37:21

The wicked borrows but does not pay back, but the righteous is generous and gives.

SCRIPTURE SUPPORT

Romans 13:8: *Owe no one anything, except to love each other, for the one who loves another has fulfilled the law.*

Proverbs 22:26–27: *Be not one of those who gives pledge, who put up security for debts. If you have nothing with which to pay, why should your bed be taken from under you?*

Ecclesiastes 5:5: *It is better that you should not vow than that you should vow and not pay.*

THOUGHTS TO CONSIDER

It may seem obvious to say that when you borrow money you are to repay it, however, one aspect we take for granted is that our payments are set to be made in the future. Can anyone guarantee the future? Solomon provides us valuable wisdom when he says, *"Since no one knows the future, who can tell someone else what is to come"* (Eccles. 8:7). So, when borrowing, we are setting ourselves up to make payments in an unknown future. Accordingly, we need to ask ourselves, "Will I be able to make the payments due on this debt in the future, which is required of me?" Consider the situation before taking on an obligation of future payments.

BIBLE STUDY
James 4:13-17

BIBLE STUDY QUESTIONS

1. Who was James talking to?

2. What questions does James pose to the people?

3. The questions James asked may be rhetorical, but he provides his reasons for asking. What reasons were given to the people?

4. What does James say we should do?

5. What does James say we do that is evil?

6. How does our evil boasting relate back to our paying debts?

Answers: Page 276

Greed

Question 49:

What is greed?

ANSWER:

Greed is the selfish desire to continue to accumulate money and possessions beyond what we currently have.

 MEMORY VERSE

ECCLESIASTES 5:10

He who loves money will not be satisfied with money, nor he who loves wealth with his income; this also is vanity.

SCRIPTURE SUPPORT

Colossians 3:5: *Put to death therefore what is earthly in you: sexual immorality, impurity, passion, evil desire, and covetousness, which is idolatry.*

Luke 12:15: *And he said to them, "Take care, and be on your guard against all covetousness, for one's life does not consist in the abundance of his possessions."*

1 John 2:16: *For all that is in the world—the desires of the flesh and the desires of the eyes and pride of life—is not from the Father but is from the world.*

THOUGHTS TO CONSIDER

After exploring the biblical concepts of money throughout this book, we can see how and why greed is so dangerous. Greed can only enter our life when we look at financial possessions as our own. When we view ourselves as stewards, the act of accumulating more should not be an issue because we are merely managing what is given to us.

BIBLE STUDY
1 Kings 21

BIBLE STUDY QUESTIONS

1. What did Ahab want that was close to his palace?

2. What did Ahab offer Naboth?

3. What was Naboth's response?

4. How did Ahab respond to Naboth?

5. What happened when Ahab told his wife, Jezebel, about his dealings with Naboth?

6. What did Elijah say to Ahab when he met Ahab at Naboth's vineyard?

7. After looking at this scenario, what can greed do in our lives?

Answers: Page 278

Question 50:

What are the consequences of greed?

ANSWER:

The Lord disciplines us when we are greedy to teach us a lesson.

MEMORY VERSE

PROVERBS 15:27

Whoever is greedy for unjust gain troubles his own household, but he who hates bribes will live.

SCRIPTURE SUPPORT

Numbers 11:34: *Therefore the name of that place was called Kibroth-hattaavah, because there they buried the people who had the craving.*

Jeremiah 6:12–13: *"Their houses shall be turned over to others, their fields and wives together, for I will stretch out my hand against the inhabitants of the land," declares the Lord. "For from the least to the greatest of them, everyone is greedy for unjust gain; and from prophet to priest, everyone deals falsely."*

1 Corinthians 10:6: *Now these things took place as examples for us, that we might not desire evil as they did.*

THOUGHTS TO CONSIDER

Recall that greed only occurs when we desire to continue to accumulate material wealth. There are a few reasons why we do this: 1) we think of money as our own, 2) our dependence is on our wealth for our sustainment and thus we strive to have more, and 3) greed is never satisfied so the acts to stop accumulating will never cease. Greed is something that can never be satisfied, we will always want more and, as mentioned in the previous discussion, greed can put us in situations where we do evil things to try and satisfy our greed.

BIBLE STUDY
Colossians 3:1-6

BIBLE STUDY QUESTIONS

1. What does Paul instruct those in Colossae since they have been raised in Christ?

2. In addition to our hearts, what else are we to set on things above? Why?

3. What advice does Paul give to the church in Colossae?

4. What does Paul call earthly-natured behaviors?

5. What reason does Paul give for why we should give up earthly-natured behaviors?

6. What impact does Paul's words have on you?

Answers: Page 281

Question 51:

What does greed lead to in our spiritual lives?

ANSWER:

Greed leads us away from the Lord.

 MEMORY VERSE

PSALM 10:3–4

For the wicked boasts of the desires of his soul, and the one greedy for gain curses and renounces the Lord. In the pride of his face the wicked does not seek him; all his thoughts are, "There is no God."

SCRIPTURE SUPPORT

Romans 1: 28–29: *And since they did not see fit to acknowledge God, God gave them up to a debased mind to do what ought not to be done. They were filled with all manner of unrighteousness, evil, covetousness, malice. They are full of envy, murder, strife, deceit, maliciousness. They are gossips*

Proverbs 28:25: *A greedy man stirs up strife, but the one who trusts in the Lord will be enriched.*

Matthew 6:24: *No one can serve two masters. Either you will hate the one and love the other, or you will be devoted to the one and despise the other. You cannot serve both God and money.*

THOUGHTS TO CONSIDER

As soon as greedy intentions come into our minds (and we begin to act upon them), we immediately are turning away from God and seeking to better our own position. We must always remember that in the eyes of the Lord, the *"last will be first and the first will be last"* (Matt. 19:30). We need to continually be mindful of our human tendency to seek after possessions and the desire for more and more, as well as the resulting impact on our spiritual lives when we act on those desires.

BIBLE STUDY
Ezekiel 14:1-8

BIBLE STUDY QUESTIONS

1. What response did God give to the Priest/Prophet Ezekiel when some of the elders came to inquire of him?

2. What did God tell Ezekiel he would do to Israelites who were idolizers?

3. What was Ezekiel instructed to tell the people of Israel?

4. What happened if any Israelite or foreigner inquired of a prophet with idols in their hearts?

5. How does God's response to idolization inform us about his character toward greed?

Answers: Page 282

Question 52:

What if we are consistently tempted by greed?

ANSWER:

When we are tempted by greed, we need to seek out our faithful God.

 MEMORY VERSE

1 Corinthians 10:13

No temptation has overtaken you except what is common to mankind. And God is faithful; he will not let you be tempted beyond what you can bear. But when you are tempted, he will also provide a way out so that you can endure it.

SCRIPTURE SUPPORT

Proverbs 16:32: *Better a patient person than a warrior, one with self-control than on who takes a city.*

Psalm 73:25: *Whom have I in Heaven but you? And there is nothing on earth that I desire besides you.*

Mark 11:24: *"Therefore I tell you, whatever you ask in prayer, believe that you have received it, and it will be yours."*

THOUGHTS TO CONSIDER

If we think that greed may be an issue, either now or later, the best solution is the same advice that Ezekiel gave the Israelites: *to repent* (Ezek. 14). Also, we are to believe in the work and worth of Jesus Christ.

As you have gone through this guide, our prayer is that you have drawn closer to God and that if you have not fully put your trust and faith in him, and him alone, you will take time right now to commit your life to Christ.

This question will not have the Bible Study or Bible Study Questions sections which are replaced with Bible Verses and Prayer to help guide you, your family, and or friends to hear the Word of God in anticipation that the Holy Spirit will help one and all to realize our total depravity and need for a savior.

BIBLE VERSES

Romans 3:23: *for all have sinned and fall short of the glory of God,*

Romans 6:23: *For the wages of sin is death, but the free gift of God is eternal life in Christ Jesus our Lord.*

Romans 5:8: *But God demonstrates His own love toward us, in that while we were yet sinners, Christ died for us.*

John 3:16: *"For God so loved the world, that He gave His only begotten Son, that whoever believes in Him shall not perish, but have eternal life."*

Romans 10:9: *that if you confess with your mouth Jesus as Lord, and believe in your heart that God raised Him from the dead, you will be saved;*

1 John 1:9: *If we confess our sins, He is faithful and righteous to forgive us our sins and to cleanse us from all unrighteousness.*

John 1:12: *But as many as received Him, to them He gave the right to become children of God, even to those who believe in His name,*

Ephesians 2:8–9: *For by grace you have been saved through faith; and that not of yourselves, it is the gift of God; not as a result of works, so that no one may boast.*

2 Corinthians 5:17: *Therefore if anyone is in Christ, he is a new creature; the old things passed away; behold, new things have come.*

Ephesians 1:7: *In Him we have redemption through His blood, the forgiveness of our trespasses, according to the riches of His grace.*

Prayer

Heavenly Father,

May your Word rest upon us as we read these verses. May the act of hearing your words prompt us to acknowledge that we are sinners and have rebelled against your perfect ways. You, and you alone, provide new mercies and grace each day through our new and revitalized faith in your son, Christ Jesus. For as we read, it was by his death and your gift of grace—not by our works—that allows us to be called your children, heirs with Christ, your son.

Lord, we pray that those reciting (and hearing) this prayer accept and acknowledge we are all sinners and have need to repent, to turn away from our sinful nature, and believe in the work and worth of Jesus Christ. Allow the Holy Spirit to lead us each day as we strive to know you more, seek the things of your divine nature, and become a new creature. May this book be used as a tool to continually guide us to repentance and faith in Christ.

Amen.

BEYOND OUR
BIBLICAL
WORLDVIEW

Whether you are an individual, couple, family, small group, or accountability partners you may have come to the realization that knowing a biblical worldview of money is far easier than "living" out that same worldview. There are many reasons for this, such as the natural inclinations of our sinful nature or perhaps the influx and allure of commercials and advertisements that tell us we need more. Regardless of the reason, seeking to live our lives in a way that aligns with our beliefs can be impossible if left to our own accord.

The following additional questions are not included in the 52 weekly devotions, but it is important to leave you with how best to continue your faithful journey of money management from a biblical worldview. These last two questions are outlined in the same manner as the book so that you can explore Scripture memory, contemplation, and Bible Study Questions.

Supplemental Question 1:

If money is so important to God, how do we get help?

ANSWER:

Seeking counsel will give us wisdom.

 MEMORY VERSE

PROVERBS 12:15

The way of a fool is right in his own eyes, but a wise man listens to advice.

SCRIPTURE SUPPORT

Proverbs 1:5: *Let the wise hear and increase in learning, and the one who understands obtain guidance.*

Proverbs 13:10: *By insolence comes nothing but strife, but with those who take advice is wisdom.*

Proverbs 19:20: *Listen to advice and accept instruction, that you may gain wisdom in the future.*

THOUGHTS TO CONSIDER

"No one is righteous, no not one" (Rom. 3:10). We need to remember that we probably cannot manage God's resources fully on our own. We need to seek out counsel, specifically counsel from biblically mature individuals. How do you know who is biblically mature? The Holy Spirit will guide you but you can always follow the great advice Paul gives to that of an elder in the church. They must be above reproach, *"faithful to his wife, temperate, self-controlled, respectable, hospitable, able to teach, not given to drunkenness, not violent but gentle, not quarrelsome, not a lover of money"* (1 Tim. 3:2–3).

BIBLE STUDY
2 Chronicles 1

BIBLE STUDY QUESTIONS

1. How does 2 Chronicles 1 begin?

2. As Solomon offered burnt offerings at the bronze altar in the tent of meeting, what happened?

3. What did Solomon reply?

4. How did God respond to Solomon?

5. What else does God give to Solomon?

6. What makes this request so pleasing to God?

Answers: Page 284

Supplemental Question 2:

How should we seek biblical counsel?

> **ANSWER:**
>
> It is best to get input from multiple wise counselors.

 MEMORY VERSE

PROVERBS 15:22

Without counsel plans fail, but with many advisers they succeed.

SCRIPTURE SUPPORT

Proverbs 11:14: *Where there is no guidance, a people falls, but in an abundance of counselors there is safety.*

Proverbs 15:31–33: *The ear that listens to life-giving reproof will dwell among the wise. Whoever ignores instruction despises himself, but he who listens to reproof gains intelligence. The fear of the Lord is instruction in wisdom, and humility comes before honor.*

Proverbs 24:5–6: *A wise man is full of strength, and a man of knowledge enhances his might, for by wise guidance you can wage your war, and in abundance of counselors there is victory.*

THOUGHTS TO CONSIDER

Biblical counsel we receive from others should be an important consideration in our decision-making. However, when we receive wise counsel, we must also consider the teachings of Scripture, our personal experience, and discernment of the Holy Spirit's teaching through prayer as well. By seeking biblical counsel from a variety of sources, we can begin to gain a more comprehensive understanding of the issue/scenario and the potential outcomes. We may decide to allow certain individuals in our life to have a stronger influence in regards to the wisdom we seek, but it is probably still best to gather different perspectives. The beauty of God's design is that God gives us at least three immediate sources for guidance: family (especially parents), church family, and the Holy Spirit.

BIBLE STUDY

1 Kings 2:1-4 and Proverbs 1:8-9; 6:20-22; 23:22

BIBLE STUDY QUESTIONS

1. What are some of the qualifications that make parents a great resource for biblical counsel?

2. According to Proverbs 6:20–22, what will our father's and mother's instructions do for us?

3. What sound counsel did David give to Solomon on his deathbed?

4. How can you and your family set up a method of communication such that the children can openly seek the counsel of the parents?

*Use the "Family Meeting Agenda" as a guide for your family meetings. (Refer to Appendix B.)

Answers: Page 286

SUMMARY

If you are reading this, then you have likely completed all of the financial discipline readings. Congratulations! That is a great accomplishment. I hope that this book has helped lay a sound biblical framework for you, your children and others with whom you may have shared this study, as it relates to managing money God's way. My recommendation would be to go back through the questions and answers frequently. Recall the words of Moses to the Israelites: *"These commandments that I give you today are to be on your hearts. Impress them on your children. Talk about them when you sit at home and when you walk along the road, when you lie down and when you get up"'* (Deut. 6:6–7 NIV).

If I can be of any help, please feel free to email me any questions or comments you have. Additionally, I would love to hear any testimonies on how this book has been encouraging, engaging, and equipping for you and your family.

May God continue to be with you.

God Bless,

Justin

justinhenegar@gmail.com

APPENDIX A:
PASTOR INTERVIEW

1. As a pastor, how has your view of money changed over the years?

_____

_____

_____

2. What Bible verses have impacted you the most as it relates to money or money management?

_____

_____

_____

3. As a pastor, what types of issues do you see with Christians as it relates to money?

_____

_____

_____

4. What general advice do you give to people seeking financial help?

_____

_____

_____

5. As I prepare to start managing money (God's resources), what top three (3) financial tips or advices would you give someone my age?

_____

_____

_____

APPENDIX B:
FAMILY MEETING AGENDA

Henegar Meeting Agenda (example)   Date:

Step 1: Open the meeting in Prayer

Step 2: Review last week's notes and update everyone on circumstances that were addressed in previous meetings.

Step 3: Each person gets at least **3 minutes** to discuss their day / week / month and address the following items:

- What obstacles have they encountered?
  - Mom
  - Dad
  - Child 1
  - Child 2
  - Child 3
  - Child 4

- What concerns do they have with others in the household?
  - Mom
  - Dad
  - Child 1
  - Child 2
  - Child 3
  - Child 4

- What ideas or solutions can they come up with to address problems?
  - Mom
  - Dad
  - Child 1
  - Child 2
  - Child 3
  - Child 4

- What goals or action items would they like to complete before the next meeting?
  - Mom
  - Dad
  - Child 1
  - Child 2
  - Child 3
  - Child 4

Step 5: End in prayer

One person in the family needs to be the "recorder" of the meeting and it would be recommended that this job be rotated amongst all family members that are capable of fulfilling this responsibility.

BIBLE STUDY QUESTION ANSWER GUIDE

GOD'S OWNERSHIP

QUESTION 1 ANSWERS:
WHAT DOES GOD OWN?

Bible Study
Deuteronomy 10:12-22

¹² And now, Israel, what doth Jehovah thy God require of thee, but to fear Jehovah thy God, to walk in all his ways, and to love him, and to serve Jehovah thy God with all thy heart and with all thy soul, ¹³ to keep the commandments of Jehovah, and his statutes, which I command thee this day for thy good? ¹⁴ Behold, unto Jehovah thy God belongeth heaven and the heaven of heavens, the earth, with all that is therein. ¹⁵ Only Jehovah had a delight in thy fathers to love them, and he chose their seed after them, even you above all peoples, as at this day. ¹⁶ Circumcise therefore the foreskin of your heart, and be no more stiffnecked. ¹⁷ For Jehovah your God, he is God of gods, and Lord of lords, the great God, the mighty, and the terrible, who regardeth not persons, nor taketh reward. ¹⁸ He doth execute justice for the fatherless and widow, and loveth the sojourner, in giving him food and raiment. ¹⁹ Love ye therefore the sojourner; for ye were sojourners in the land of Egypt. ²⁰ Thou shalt fear Jehovah thy

God; him shalt thou serve; and to him shalt thou cleave, and by his name shalt thou swear. [21] He is thy praise, and he is thy God, that hath done for thee these great and terrible things, which thine eyes have seen. [22] Thy fathers went down into Egypt with threescore and ten persons; and now Jehovah thy God hath made thee as the stars of heaven for multitude.

Bible Study Questions and Answers

1. What five things does God require of his people?
   a. Fear the Lord
   b. Walk in his ways
   c. Love him
   d. Serve him with all your heart and soul
   e. Keep his commandments and statutes

2. Although God owns everything, what did God do?
   God has established us, those called according to Jesus Christ to be his people.

3. How does Deuteronomy 10:14 inform our understanding of what God is asking for in verse 10:16 when he tells the Israelites to circumcise their hearts and to no longer be stiffnecked?
   We should not hold on to our money as our own. To be stubborn means to not change our attitude or position in spite of good reasons to do so.

4. What does God do to those who have very little (i.e., fatherless, widow, sojourner)?
   God brings justice for those with very little and provides their basic necessities, such as food and water.

5. Knowing that God owns everything, what are we to do for sojourners?
   We are to love sojourners and provide for their needs (food and clothing).

6. How does having a perspective that God owns everything change our thoughts about money?*
   When we stop to think about God's ownership, it should change our entire life. Everything we see, touch, feel, all

comes from the Lord. If it is not ours, then we need to ac-knowledge that it all belongs to him and then, most impor-tantly, we need to determine what the Lord wants us to do with his money. When we understand that God is the owner of everything, we begin to handle our money and possessions differently, in a more responsible way. We tend to be more cautious, careful, and considerate of other people's posses-sions than we do with our own.

*Individual responses may vary.

QUESTION 2 ANSWERS:
IF GOD OWNS EVERYTHING, WHAT IS OUR ROLE?

Bible Study
Genesis 39:1-6

And Joseph was brought down to Egypt; and Potiphar, an officer of Pha-raoh's, the captain of the guard, an Egyptian, bought him of the hand of the Ishmaelites, that had brought him down thither. ² And Jehovah was with Jo-seph, and he was a prosperous man; and he was in the house of his master the Egyptian. ³ And his master saw that Jehovah was with him, and that Jehovah made all that he did to prosper in his hand. ⁴ And Joseph found favor in his sight, and he ministered unto him: and he made him overseer over his house, and all that he had he put into his hand. ⁵ And it came to pass from the time that he made him overseer in his house, and over all that he had, that Jehovah blessed the Egyptian's house for Joseph's sake; and the blessing of Jehovah was upon all that he had, in the house and in the field. ⁶ And he left all that he had in Joseph's hand; and he knew not aught that was with him, save the bread which he did eat. And Joseph was comely, and well-favored.

Bible Study Questions

1. Who are the main characters?
   a. Joseph
   b. Potiphar
   c. God

2. How did Potiphar view Joseph?

   Joseph found favor in his sight.

3. Based on how Potiphar viewed Joseph, what did he do?

   Potiphar made Joseph an overseer of his house and put him in charge of all that he had.

4. Once Potiphar put Joseph in charge of his household, how did Potiphar feel?

   Potiphar had no concern about anything (except the food he ate).

5. Think about a time when you were allowed to use something that belonged to someone else. How did you handle what you were given? If you handled it differently, why?*

   Think of a time when you were allowed to use something that wasn't your own (perhaps you borrowed someone's car). How did you drive? You likely drove very careful. Do you always drive that carefully when you drive your own car? There may be other examples. As we realize God owns everything, we need to take care of possessions as belonging to him, not as our possessions.

   *Individual answers may vary.

QUESTION 4 ANSWERS:
WHEN DOES BECOMING A STEWARD TAKE EFFECT?

Bible Study
Matthew 16:21–28

[21] From that time began Jesus to show unto his disciples, that he must go unto Jerusalem, and suffer many things of the elders and chief priests and scribes, and be killed, and the third day be raised up. [22] And Peter took him, and began to rebuke him, saying, "Be it far from thee, Lord: this shall never be unto thee." [23] But he turned, and said unto Peter, "Get thee behind me, Satan: thou art a stumbling-block unto me: for thou mindest not the things of God, but the things of men." [24] Then said Jesus unto his disciples, "If any man would come after me, let him deny himself, and take up his cross, and follow me. [25]

For whosoever would save his life shall lose it: and whosoever shall lose his life for my sake shall find it. ²⁶ For what shall a man be profited, if he shall gain the whole world, and forfeit his life? or what shall a man give in exchange for his life? ²⁷For the Son of man shall come in the glory of his Father with his angels; and then shall he render unto every man according to his deeds. ²⁸ "Verily I say unto you, 'There are some of them that stand here, who shall in no wise taste of death, till they see the Son of man coming in his kingdom.'"

Bible Study Questions and Answers

1. What was Jesus' response to Simon Peter when he tried to rebuke him?

   Jesus responded, *"Get behind me, Satan! You are a hindrance to me. For you are not setting your mind on the things of God, but on the things of man"* (Matt. 16:23).

2. When we think that we own our material possessions, are our thoughts on the things of God or the things of man? Why?*

   When we feel ownership of material possessions, our thoughts will typically be on what those possessions can do for us and how we can improve our own position, which prohibits us from setting our mind on the things of God.

3. How can we transition from thinking about the things of man to thinking about the things of God?

   We each need to pursue Jesus, deny our self, and take up our cross and follow Christ. The key here is to 'deny our self' which implies we sacrifice our time and resources for the sake of Christ.

4. As you think about God's ownership of all that you possess, do you feel that you have relinquished ownership of your possessions?*

   This can be challenging to truly answer. Keep in mind your attitude toward your possessions. Do you feel negative emotions such as anxiety, frustration, anger, or uneasy when you think about God taking anything of "yours" away. Reflecting on your feelings will be a good indicator.

*Individual responses may vary.

QUESTION 5 ANSWERS:
WHAT DOES A STEWARD RECEIVE FOR THEIR WORK?

Bible Study
Genesis 22

And it came to pass after these things, that God did prove Abraham, and said unto him, "Abraham"; and he said, "Here am I." ² And he said, "Take now thy son, thine only son, whom thou lovest, even Isaac, and get thee into the land of Moriah; and offer him there for a burnt offering upon one of the mountains which I will tell thee of." ³ And Abraham rose early in the morning, and saddled his ass, and took two of his young men with him, and Isaac his son; and he clave the wood for the burnt offering, and rose up, and went unto the place of which God had told him. ⁴ On the third day Abraham lifted up his eyes, and saw the place afar off. ⁵ And Abraham said unto his young men, "Abide ye here with the ass, and I and the lad will go yonder; and we will worship, and come again to you." ⁶ And Abraham took the wood of the burnt offering, and laid it upon Isaac his son; and he took in his hand the fire and the knife; and they went both of them together. ⁷ And Isaac spake unto Abraham his father, and said, "My father": and he said, "Here am I, my son." And he said, "Behold, the fire and the wood: but where is the lamb for a burnt offering?" ⁸ And Abraham said, "God will provide himself the lamb for a burnt offering, my son: so they went both of them together."

⁹ And they came to the place which God had told him of; and Abraham built the altar there, and laid the wood in order, and bound Isaac his son, and laid him on the altar, upon the wood. ¹⁰ And Abraham stretched forth his hand, and took the knife to slay his son. ¹¹ And the angel of Jehovah called unto him out of heaven, and said, "Abraham, Abraham": and he said, "Here am I." ¹² And he said, "Lay not thy hand upon the lad, neither do thou anything unto him; for now I know that thou fearest God, seeing thou hast not withheld thy son, thine only son, from me." ¹³ And Abraham lifted up his eyes, and looked, and, behold, behind him a ram caught in the thicket by his horns: and Abraham went and took the ram, and offered him up for a burnt offering in the stead of his son. ¹⁴ And Abraham called the name of that place Jehovah-Jireh: as it is said to this day, In the mount of Jehovah it shall be provided. ¹⁵ And

the angel of Jehovah called unto Abraham a second time out of heaven, [16] and said, "By myself have I sworn, saith Jehovah, because thou hast done this thing, and hast not withheld thy son, thine only son, [17] that in blessing I will bless thee, and in multiplying I will multiply thy seed as the stars of the heavens, and as the sand which is upon the seashore; and thy seed shall possess the gate of his enemies; [18] and in thy seed shall all the nations of the earth be blessed; because thou hast obeyed my voice." [19] So Abraham returned unto his young men, and they rose up and went together to Beersheba; and Abraham dwelt at Beersheba.

[20] And it came to pass after these things, that it was told Abraham, saying, "Behold, Milcah, she also hath borne children unto thy brother Nahor: [21] Uz his firstborn, and Buz his brother, and Kemuel the father of Aram, [22] and Chesed, and Hazo, and Pildash, and Jidlaph, and Bethuel. [23] And Bethuel begat Rebekah: these eight did Milcah bear to Nahor, Abraham's brother. [24] And his concubine, whose name was Reumah, she also bare Tebah, and Gaham, and Tahash, and Maacah."

Bible Study Questions and Answers

1. Who are the characters in this story?
   a. Abraham
   b. Abraham's son, Isaac
   c. God
   d. Two servants of Abraham
   e. Angel of the Lord

2. What did God ask Abraham to do?
   God told Abraham to take Isaac to Moriah and sacrifice him there as a burnt offering.

3. When did Abraham act on the task commanded by God?
   Abraham got up early the next morning in his faithfulness.

4. Refer to Genesis 22:10. Why was Abraham's response to God's command so important in light of being a steward?*
   Abraham looked at what he had as God's and believed in God (Rom. 4:3). This faith in God dominated his life, even beyond his most prized possession, Isaac.

5. Reread Genesis 22:15–18. What did the Lord say (and do) to Abraham?

> The Lord told Abraham that he would bless him and bless his descendants, and that through him all nations would be blessed.

*Individual answers may vary.

STEWARDSHIP

QUESTION 6 ANSWERS:
HOW DO WE GET THE THINGS WE HAVE?

Bible Study
Matthew 6:19-34

[19] Lay not up for yourselves treasures upon the earth, where moth and rust consume, and where thieves break through and steal: [20] but lay up for yourselves treasures in heaven, where neither moth nor rust doth consume, and where thieves do not break through nor steal: [21] for where thy treasure is, there will thy heart be also. [22] The lamp of the body is the eye: if therefore thine eye be single, thy whole body shall be full of light. [23] But if thine eye be evil, thy whole body shall be full of darkness. If therefore the light that is in thee be darkness, how great is the darkness! [24] No man can serve two masters: for either he will hate the one, and love the other; or else he will hold to one, and despise the other. Ye cannot serve God and mammon. [25] Therefore I say unto you, Be not anxious for your life, what ye shall eat, or what ye shall drink; nor yet for your body, what ye shall put on. Is not the life more than the food, and the body than the raiment? [26] Behold the birds of the heaven, that they sow not, neither do they reap, nor gather into barns; and your heavenly Father feedeth them. Are not ye of much more value than they? [27] And which of you by being anxious can add one cubit unto the measure of his life? [28] And why are ye anxious concerning raiment? Consider the lilies of the field, how

they grow; they toil not, neither do they spin: [29] yet I say unto you, that even Solomon in all his glory was not arrayed like one of these. [30] But if God doth so clothe the grass of the field, which today is, and tomorrow is cast into the oven, shall he not much more clothe you, O ye of little faith? [31] Be not therefore anxious, saying, What shall we eat? or, What shall we drink? or, Wherewithal shall we be clothed? [32] For after all these things do the Gentiles seek; for your heavenly Father knoweth that ye have need of all these things. [33] But seek ye first his kingdom, and his righteousness; and all these things shall be added unto you. [34] Be not therefore anxious for the morrow: for the morrow will be anxious for itself. Sufficient unto the day is the evil thereof.

Bible Study Questions and Answers

1. What does Jesus instruct us to do in the first part of his monologue?
   Jesus tells us to start putting our treasure in the things of Heaven and not in those things on earth because things on the earth will be destroyed.

2. What specific emotion is addressed by Jesus?
   Jesus says that we are not to be anxious.

3. What reason does Jesus offer the audience to assure them of provision?
   Our Lord God provides for the least of his creation (ravens) and since we are so much more valuable than the ravens, he will provide for us even more.

4. What does Jesus say the Gentiles seek after?
   Food, drink, and clothes are sought after by the Gentiles.

5. What does Jesus say that Christians should seek after?
   We Christians are first to seek after God and his righteousness and then God will provide what we need, i.e., our food, drink, and clothes.

QUESTION 7 ANSWERS:
HOW MUCH DOES GOD GIVE US?

Bible Study
Luke 9:1-6; 22:35-37

Luke 9:1-6

And he called the twelve together, and gave them power and authority over all demons, and to cure diseases. ²And he sent them forth to preach the kingdom of God, and to heal the sick. ³And he said unto them, "Take nothing for your journey, neither staff, nor wallet, nor bread, nor money; neither have two coats. ⁴And into whatsoever house ye enter, there abide, and thence depart. ⁵And as many as receive you not, when ye depart from that city, shake off the dust from your feet for a testimony against them." ⁶And they departed, and went throughout the villages, preaching the gospel, and healing everywhere.

Luke 22:35-37

And he said unto them, "When I sent you forth without purse, and wallet, and shoes, lacked ye anything?" And they said, "Nothing." ³⁶And he said unto them, "But now, he that hath a purse, let him take it, and likewise a wallet; and he that hath none, let him sell his cloak, and buy a sword. ³⁷For I say unto you, that this which is written must be fulfilled in me, 'And he was reckoned with transgressors: for that which concerneth me hath fulfilment.'"

Bible Study Questions and Answers

1. What is happening at this point in Jesus' ministry?
   Jesus is sending out his disciples two by two to preach the good news.

2. What did Jesus give to his disciples before he sent them out?
   Jesus gave them power and authority over all demons and to cure diseases.

3. After Jesus gave the disciples authority, what did he command them to take?

> The disciples were commanded to take nothing on their journey.

4. Why did Jesus not allow the disciples to take any necessities or money to buy necessities on their journey?*

> One thought is that Jesus wanted his disciples to learn to trust him to provide when they were without any necessities so that they would also trust him when they did have them. When our life's necessities are limited or non-existence, we tend to exhibit maximum faith.

5. Refer to Luke 22:35–37. What did Jesus ask the disciples? What was their response?

> Jesus asked them if they lacked anything when they were sent out and their response was they did not lack anything.

6. Do you believe that we must first go through a faith strengthening exercise like that of the disciples before we can use God's resources and keep our stronghold faith?*

> Not necessarily. God moves people in different ways. It is helpful to have accountability in our stewardship journey, though, because God does use various circumstances in our lives to test our faithfulness to him. By going through trying situations, one can learn to truly trust the Lord to provide.

*Individual answers may vary.

QUESTION 8 ANSWERS:
IF WE TRUST IN GOD, WILL HE FINANCIALLY BLESS US?

Bible Study
1 Kings 17:7–16

[7] And it came to pass after a while, that the brook dried up, because there was no rain in the land. [8] And the word of Jehovah came unto him, saying, [9] "Arise, get thee to Zarephath, which belongeth to Sidon, and dwell there: behold, I

have commanded a widow there to sustain thee." ¹⁰ So he arose and went to Zarephath; and when he came to the gate of the city, behold, a widow was there gathering sticks: and he called to her, and said, "Fetch me, I pray thee, a little water in a vessel, that I may drink." ¹¹ And as she was going to fetch it, he called to her, and said, "Bring me, I pray thee, a morsel of bread in thy hand." ¹² And she said, "As Jehovah thy God liveth, I have not a cake, but a handful of meal in the jar, and a little oil in the cruse: and, behold, I am gathering two sticks, that I may go in and dress it for me and my son, that we may eat it, and die." ¹³ And Elijah said unto her, "Fear not; go and do as thou hast said; but make me thereof a little cake first, and bring it forth unto me, and afterward make for thee and for thy son." ¹⁴ For thus saith Jehovah, the God of Israel, "'The jar of meal shall not waste, neither shall the cruse of oil fail, until the day that Jehovah sendeth rain upon the earth.'" ¹⁵ And she went and did according to the saying of Elijah: and she, and he, and her house, did eat many days. ¹⁶ The jar of meal wasted not, neither did the cruse of oil fail, according to the word of Jehovah, which he spake by Elijah.

Bible Study Questions and Answers

1. Who are the characters in 1 Kings 17:7–16?
    a. Elijah
    b. a widow
    c. the widow's son

2. Where did God command Elijah to go and what was Elijah expecting to receive when he got there?
    Elijah was to go to Zarephath. God told Elijah that he would direct a widow to take care of him by providing him food.

3. What was the widow's reply to Elijah when he asked her to bring him a piece of bread? And what was Elijah's response to her?
    The widow told Elijah she didn't have any bread and that she only had enough supplies to make one last meal for her and her son. Elijah told her to not be afraid and to go about making the bread. He asked her to make him a small loaf, bring it to him and next to make a loaf for her and her son.

4. What did Elijah say to her on behalf of the Lord?

   That her supplies (the jar of flour and the jug of oil) would not be emptied until the Lord sends rain.

5. Even though the widow had only enough for one last meal, what do you think inspired her to do what Elijah said, knowing her circumstances were so dire?*

   Elijah was a prophet and was probably known around the area as a man of God. Speaking on behalf of God, the widow was given the promise that her flour and oil would not run out. The widow acted out her faith in believing this promise. The widow's faithfulness was rewarded by seeing a miracle in her life.

   *Individual responses may vary.

QUESTION 9 ANSWERS:
CAN GOD TAKE AWAY WHAT HE HAS GIVEN TO US?

Bible Study
Job 1:1–22

There was a man in the land of Uz, whose name was Job; and that man was perfect and upright, and one that feared God, and turned away from evil. [2] And there were born unto him seven sons and three daughters. [3] His substance also was seven thousand sheep, and three thousand camels, and five hundred yoke of oxen, and five hundred she asses, and a very great household; so that this man was the greatest of all the children of the east. [4] And his sons went and held a feast in the house of each one upon his day; and they sent and called for their three sisters to eat and to drink with them. [5] And it was so, when the days of their feasting were gone about, that Job sent and sanctified them, and rose up early in the morning, and offered burnt offerings according to the number of them all: for Job said, "It may be that my sons have sinned, and renounced God in their hearts." Thus did Job continually. [6] Now it came to pass on the day when the sons of God came to present themselves before Jehovah, that Satan also came among them.

7 And Jehovah said unto Satan, "Whence comest thou?" Then Satan answered Jehovah, and said, "From going to and fro in the earth, and from walking up and down in it." 8 And Jehovah said unto Satan, "Hast thou considered my servant Job? for there is none like him in the earth, a perfect and an upright man, one that feareth God, and turneth away from evil." 9 Then Satan answered Jehovah, and said, "Doth Job fear God for nought? 10 Hast not thou made a hedge about him, and about his house, and about all that he hath, on every side? thou hast blessed the work of his hands, and his substance is increased in the land. 11 But put forth thy hand now, and touch all that he hath, and he will renounce thee to thy face." 12 And Jehovah said unto Satan, "Behold, all that he hath is in thy power; only upon himself put not forth thy hand." So Satan went forth from the presence of Jehovah.

13 And it fell on a day when his sons and his daughters were eating and drinking wine in their eldest brother's house, 14 that there came a messenger unto Job, and said, "The oxen were plowing, and the asses feeding beside them; 15 and the Sabeans fell upon them, and took them away: yea, they have slain the servants with the edge of the sword; and I only am escaped alone to tell thee." 16 While he was yet speaking, there came also another, and said, "The fire of God is fallen from heaven, and hath burned up the sheep and the servants, and consumed them; and I only am escaped alone to tell thee." 17 While he was yet speaking, there came also another, and said, "The Chaldeans made three bands, and fell upon the camels, and have taken them away, yea, and slain the servants with the edge of the sword; and I only am escaped alone to tell thee." 18 While he was yet speaking, there came also another, and said, "Thy sons and thy daughters were eating and drinking wine in their eldest brother's house; 19 and, behold, there came a great wind from the wilderness, and smote the four corners of the house, and it fell upon the young men, and they are dead; and I only am escaped alone to tell thee."

20 Then Job arose, and rent his robe, and shaved his head, and fell down upon the ground, and worshipped; 21 and he said, "Naked came I out of my mother's womb, and naked shall I return thither: Jehovah gave, and Jehovah hath taken away; blessed be the name of Jehovah." 22 In all this Job sinned not, nor charged God foolishly.

Bible Study Questions and Answers

1. What were some of the characteristics used to describe Job?
   a. Job was blameless and upright.
   b. He was one who feared God.
   c. He turned away from evil.

2. What was Job doing for his children after their feasts?
   Job interceded for them by consecrating them and sacrificed burnt offerings in case they had sinned.

3. What reasons did Satan give to the Lord that justified Job's righteousness?
   The Lord
   a. protected Job (put a hedge around him).
   b. protected all that Job had.
   c. blessed the work of Job's hands.
   d. allowed for an increase in his possessions.

4. What did Satan suggest the Lord do that would make Job curse the Lord's name?
   Satan suggested that the Lord take away all Job had.

5. To prove Job's righteousness, what did the Lord allow Satan to do to him? Were there any conditions?
   a. Satan was allowed to take all that Job had.
   b. Satan was not allowed to do anything to Job physically.

6. As you think about the first part of the story of Job, what is to be our attitude regarding what we have?*
   We should look at what God has given us with a gracious and humble attitude. Also, we ought always hold the possessions God allows us to use with an "open hand," accepting that God may put more in our hands or take things away. We also want to be very mindful to not "close our hand" so that we begin to think of God's resources as our own.

*Individual responses may vary.

QUESTION 10 ANSWERS:
WHAT HAPPENS IF WE PUT OUR TRUST IN MONEY?

Bible Study
Acts 4:32–37; 5:1–11

Acts 4:32–37

And the multitude of them that believed were of one heart and soul: and not one of them said that aught of the things which he possessed was his own; but they had all things common. ³³ And with great power gave the apostles their witness of the resurrection of the Lord Jesus: and great grace was upon them all. ³⁴ For neither was there among them any that lacked: for as many as were possessors of lands or houses sold them, and brought the prices of the things that were sold, ³⁵ and laid them at the apostles' feet: and distribution was made unto each, according as any one had need. ³⁶ And Joseph, who by the apostles was surnamed Barnabas (which is, being interpreted, Son of exhortation), a Levite, a man of Cyprus by race, ³⁷ having a field, sold it, and brought the money and laid it at the apostles' feet.

Acts 5:1–11

But a certain man named Ananias, with Sapphira his wife, sold a possession, ² and kept back part of the price, his wife also being privy to it, and brought a certain part, and laid it at the apostles' feet. ³ But Peter said, Ananias, why hath Satan filled thy heart to lie to the Holy Spirit, and to keep back part of the price of the land? ⁴ While it remained, did it not remain thine own? and after it was sold, was it not in thy power? How is it that thou hast conceived this thing in thy heart? thou hast not lied unto men, but unto God. ⁵ And Ananias hearing these words fell down and gave up the ghost: and great fear came upon all that heard it. ⁶ And the young men arose and wrapped him round, and they carried him out and buried him. ⁷ And it was about the space of three hours after, when his wife, not knowing what was done, came in. ⁸ And Peter answered unto her, Tell me whether ye sold the land for so much. And she said, Yea, for so much. ⁹ But Peter said unto her, How is it that ye have agreed together to try the Spirit of the Lord? behold, the feet of them that have buried thy husband are at the door, and they shall carry thee out. [10] And she fell down immediately at his feet, and gave up the ghost: and the young men came in and found her dead, and they carried her out and buried her by her husband. [11] And great fear came upon the whole church, and upon all that heard these things.

Bible Study Questions and Answers

1. What does Acts 4:32 tell us about the people?
   They all agreed that their possessions were not their own.

2. What were these early Christians doing?
   The people were selling their possessions and giving the proceeds to the apostles for distribution to those in need to ensure the needs of others were met.

3. Ananias and Sapphira were the two main characters in Acts 5:1–11. What did they sell? Why?
   Ananias and Sapphira sold a piece of property. They had decided to support the needs of the church as other early Christians were doing.

4. What "little" thing did Ananias and Sapphira do?
   Ananias, with the knowledge of his wife, Sapphira, kept back some of the proceeds from the sale of their property for themselves.

5. While the Apostle Peter was talking to Ananias, what happened?
   Ananias fell to the ground and died.

6. What happened when Sapphira came back to talk to Peter?
   Similar to her husband, Ananias, Sapphira also lied to Peter regarding the purchase price, and she died.

7. Do you feel that the death of Ananias and Sapphira was too extreme? Why or why not?*
   Keep in mind that Ananias and Sapphira lied, not to Peter, but to God. Also recall that we read, *"Now the full number of*

those who believed were of one heart and soul, and no one said that any of the things that belonged to him was his own, but they had everything in common" (Acts 4:32). Ananias and Sapphira probably gave most of what they received from the land, but God cares so much about our heart and not about our outward expression of pleasing him.

CONTENTMENT

QUESTION 11 ANSWERS:
WHAT IS CONTENTMENT?

Bible Study
2 Corinthians 11:20-29

For ye bear with a man, if he bringeth you into bondage, if he devoureth you, if he taketh you captive, if he exalteth himself, if he smiteth you on the face. [21] I speak by way of disparagement, as though we had been weak. Yet whereinsoever any is bold (I speak in foolishness,), I am bold also. [22] Are they Hebrews? so am I. Are they Israelites? so am I. Are they the seed of Abraham? so am I. [23] Are they ministers of Christ? (I speak as one beside himself) I more; in labors more abundantly, in prisons more abundantly, in stripes above measure, in deaths oft. [24] Of the Jews five times received I forty stripes save one. [25] Thrice was I beaten with rods, once was I stoned, thrice I suffered shipwreck, a night and a day have I been in the deep; [26] in journeyings often, in perils of rivers, in perils of robbers, in perils from my countrymen, in perils from the Gentiles, in perils in the city, in perils in the wilderness, imperils in the sea, in perils among false brethren; [27] in labor and travail, in watchings often, in hunger and thirst, in fastings often, in cold and nakedness. [28] Besides those things that are without, there is that which presseth upon me daily, anxiety for all the churches. [29] Who is weak, and I am not weak? who is caused to stumble, and I burn not?

Bible Study Questions and Answers

1. Is Paul being bold? How do you know?
   Yes, Paul says that he is speaking boldly.

2. What characteristics does Paul emphasize about himself?
   Paul says that he is
   a. a Hebrew.
   b. an Israelite.
   c. an offspring of Abraham.
   d. a servant of Christ.

3. What punishments does Paul describe in his letter to the Corinthians?
   a. Five times he received 40 lashings less 1
   b. Three times he was beaten with rods
   c. Once stoned
   d. Three times he was shipwrecked
   e. One night and one day he was adrift at sea
   f. Due to his journeys he encountered danger from:
      i. rivers
      ii. robbers
      iii. his own people
      iv. gentiles
      v. cities he was in
      vi. sea
      vii. false brothers
      viii. sleepless nights
      ix. hunger and thirst
      x. being without food
      xi. cold and exposure
      xii. self-anxiety over the church

4. In what year was 2 Corinthians thought to be written by Paul?
   A.D. 57

5. When was the letter to the Philippians written by Paul?
   A.D. 60–62

6. If Paul suffered the many perils he encountered before he wrote about learning to be content, how can we follow Paul's example?
   We need to keep in mind that God is our provider in all things and that he is a good God (Luke 12:24). When we are experiencing difficult times in our life, we can learn to be content with what we have, knowing that our precious Father will provide for our sustainment.

QUESTION 12 ANSWERS:
HOW ARE WE TO BE CONTENT?

Bible Study
Romans 9

I say the truth in Christ, I lie not, my conscience bearing witness with me in the Holy Spirit, [2] that I have great sorrow and unceasing pain in my heart. [3] For I could wish that I myself were anathema from Christ for my brethren's sake, my kinsmen according to the flesh: [4] who are Israelites; whose is the adoption, and the glory, and the covenants, and the giving of the law, and the service of God, and the promises; [5] whose are the fathers, and of whom is Christ as concerning the flesh, who is over all, God blessed for ever. Amen.

[6] But it is not as though the word of God hath come to nought. For they are not all Israel, that are of Israel: [7] neither, because they are Abraham's seed, are they all children: but, In Isaac shall thy seed be called. [8] That is, it is not the children of the flesh that are children of God; but the children of the promise are reckoned for a seed. [9] For this is a word of promise, According to this season will I come, and Sarah shall have a son. [10] And not only so; but Rebecca also having conceived by one, even by our father Isaac— [11] for the children being not yet born, neither having done anything good or bad, that the purpose of God according to election might stand, not of works, but of him that calleth, [12] it was said unto her, The elder shall serve the younger. [13] Even as it is written, Jacob I loved, but Esau I hated. [14] "What shall we say then? Is there unrighteousness with God? God forbid." [15] For he saith to Moses, "I will have mercy on whom I have mercy, and I will have compassion on whom I have compassion." [16] So then it is not of him that willeth, nor of him that runneth, but of God that hath mercy. [17] For the Scripture saith unto Pharaoh, "For this very purpose did I raise thee up, that I might show in thee my power, and that my name might be published abroad in all the earth." [18] So then he hath mercy on whom he will, and whom he will he hardeneth. [19] Thou wilt say then unto me, Why doth he still find fault? For who withstandeth his will? [20] Nay but, O man, who art thou that repliest against God? "Shall the thing formed

say to him that formed it, 'Why didst thou make me thus?'" ²¹ Or hath not the potter a right over the clay, from the same lump to make one part a vessel unto honor, and another unto dishonor? ²² What if God, willing to show his wrath, and to make his power known, endured with much longsuffering vessels of wrath fitted unto destruction: ²³ and that he might make known the riches of his glory upon vessels of mercy, which he afore prepared unto glory, ²⁴ even us, whom he also called, not from the Jews only, but also from the Gentiles? ²⁵ "As he saith also in Hosea, I will call that my people, which was not my people; And her beloved, that was not beloved." ²⁶ "And it shall be, that in the place where it was said unto them, Ye are not my people, There shall they be called sons of the living God."

²⁷ "And Isaiah crieth concerning Israel, If the number of the children of Israel be as the sand of the sea, it is the remnant that shall be saved: ²⁸ for the Lord will execute his word upon the earth, finishing it and cutting it short." ²⁹ And, as Isaiah hath said before, "Except the Lord of Sabaoth had left us a seed, We had become as Sodom, and had been made like unto Gomorrah."

³⁰ What shall we say then? That the Gentiles, who followed not after righteousness, attained to righteousness, even the righteousness which is of faith: ³¹ but Israel, following after a law of righteousness, did not arrive at that law. ³² Wherefore? Because they sought it not by faith, but as it were by works. They stumbled at the stone of stumbling; ³³ even as it is written, "Behold, I lay in Zion a stone of stumbling and a rock of offence: And he that believeth on him shall not be put to shame."

Bible Study Questions and Answers

1. What is the main theme of Romans 9?
   God's sovereign choice to do what he desires to do.

2. What major point is discussed in Romans 9:1–14?
   Man's view of who has God's favor (i.e., birth order) is not necessarily in line with God's sovereignty.

3. What promise does Paul write about that was spoken by God to Moses?

Paul proclaims that the Lord will show mercy to those he desires to show mercy and will have compassion on those whom he will have compassion.

4. What are the two challenging questions that man may ask God? What is Paul's response?
   a. Why does God still find fault? Who can resist his will?
   b. Who are we to question God? Paul gives an example of the clay questioning the potter in making them that way.

5. As you reflect on Romans 9, what do you think of the phrase, "It's not fair," when looking at what others have?*

Hopefully, we see that God has the ability to give to whomever he pleases. We need to be grateful for what he has given us. Remember that there are others that look at us and can say, "Hey, it's not fair that you have…."

*Individual answers may vary.

QUESTION 13 ANSWERS:
HOW DO WE LEARN TO BE CONTENT?

Bible Study
Philippians 4

Wherefore, my brethren beloved and longed for, my joy and crown, so stand fast in the Lord, my beloved.

² I exhort Euodia, and I exhort Syntyche, to be of the same mind in the Lord. ³ Yea, I beseech thee also, true yokefellow, help these women, for they labored with me in the gospel, with Clement also, and the rest of my fellow-workers, whose names are in the book of life.

⁴ Rejoice in the Lord always: again I will say, Rejoice. ⁵ Let your forbearance be known unto all men. The Lord is at hand. ⁶ In nothing be anxious; but in everything by prayer and supplication with thanksgiving let your requests be

made known unto God. [7] And the peace of God, which passeth all understanding, shall guard your hearts and your thoughts in Christ Jesus.

[8] Finally, brethren, whatsoever things are true, whatsoever things are honorable, whatsoever things are just, whatsoever things are pure, whatsoever things are lovely, whatsoever things are of good report; if there be any virtue, and if there be any praise, think on these things. [9] The things which ye both learned and received and heard and saw in me, these things do: and the God of peace shall be with you.

[10] But I rejoice in the Lord greatly, that now at length ye have revived your thought for me; wherein ye did indeed take thought, but ye lacked opportunity. [11] Not that I speak in respect of want: for I have learned, in whatsoever state I am, therein to be content. [12] I know how to be abased, and I know also how to abound: in everything and in all things have I learned the secret both to be filled and to be hungry, both to abound and to be in want. [13] I can do all things in him that strengtheneth me. [14] Howbeit ye did well that ye had fellowship with my affliction. [15] And ye yourselves also know, ye Philippians, that in the beginning of the gospel, when I departed from Macedonia, no church had fellowship with me in the matter of giving and receiving but ye only; [16] for even in Thessalonica ye sent once and again unto my need. [17] Not that I seek for the gift; but I seek for the fruit that increaseth to your account. [18] But I have all things, and abound: I am filled, having received from Epaphroditus the things that came from you, an odor of a sweet smell, a sacrifice acceptable, well-pleasing to God. [19] And my God shall supply every need of yours according to his riches in glory in Christ Jesus. [20] Now unto our God and Father be the glory for ever and ever. Amen.

[21] Salute every saint in Christ Jesus. The brethren that are with me salute you. [22] All the saints salute you, especially they that are of Caesar's household.

[23] The grace of the Lord Jesus Christ be with your spirit.

Bible Study Questions and Answers

1. **What does Paul ask of his readers in Philippians 4:1?**
   Stand firm in the Lord.

2. **Who were the two individuals involved in a disagreement?**
   a. Euodia
   b. Syntyche

3. **What did Paul ask the Philippians to do with the two having disagreement? Why?**
   Paul asked the Philippians to help them because Euodia and Syntyche had labored with Paul in spreading the gospel.

4. **Paul writes that we are not to be anxious about anything. How are we to do that?**
   Through prayer and supplication, with thanksgiving, we are to bring our requests to God.

5. **What does Paul's advice bring?**
   The peace of God that will guard our hearts.

6. **Paul rejoices in the Philippians' concern over him, but he also understands what about the Philippians?**
   They have not had an opportunity to physically provide for him.

7. **What has Paul learned about being in need?**
   Paul learned to be content, even in time of need, which is the secret attitude when we have sufficient resources and when we don't have enough.

8. **What is this secret Paul was proclaiming?**
   That he (and we) can do all things through our savior, Christ Jesus, because he strengthens us.

9. **How do two relatively separate issues—disagreeing and learning to live with little or with abundance—relate to contentment starting with desiring Christ?***
   Both issues—disagreeing and materialism—are grounded in the false notion that we can satisfy our own needs. Arguing

may be less obvious to us; however, because we believe we are right, it leads us to a lack of contentment as we feel the need to prove our side. Materialism makes us feel discontent because we continually seek to fulfill our desire for more, beyond what God provides for our sustainment. To be content, it is important for us to realize that we can do all things in Christ Jesus, because it is Christ who gives us strength.

*Individual answers may vary.

QUESTION 14 ANSWERS:
WHAT HAPPENS WHEN WE ARE NOT CONTENT?

Bible Study
Ecclesiastes 2

I said in my heart, "Come now, I will prove thee with mirth; therefore enjoy pleasure: and, behold, this also was vanity." ²I said of laughter, "It is mad; and of mirth, What doeth it?" ³I searched in my heart how to cheer my flesh with wine, my heart yet guiding me with wisdom, and how to lay hold on folly, till I might see what it was good for the sons of men that they should do under heaven all the days of their life. ⁴I made me great works; I builded me houses; I planted me vineyards; ⁵I made me gardens and parks, and I planted trees in them of all kinds of fruit; ⁶I made me pools of water, to water therefrom the forest where trees were reared; ⁷I bought menservants and maidservants, and had servants born in my house; also I had great possessions of herds and flocks, above all that were before me in Jerusalem; ⁸I gathered me also silver and gold, and the treasure of kings and of the provinces; I got me men singers and women singers, and the delights of the sons of men, musical instruments, and that of all sorts.

⁹So I was great, and increased more than all that were before me in Jerusalem: also my wisdom remained with me. ¹⁰And whatsoever mine eyes desired I kept not from them; I withheld not my heart from any joy; for my heart rejoiced because of all my labor; and this was my portion from all my labor. ¹¹Then I looked on all the works that my hands had wrought, and on the labor

that I had labored to do; and, behold, all was vanity and a striving after wind, and there was no profit under the sun.

[12] And I turned myself to behold wisdom, and madness, and folly: for what can the man do that cometh after the king? even that which hath been done long ago. [13] Then I saw that wisdom excelleth folly, as far as light excelleth darkness. [14] The wise man's eyes are in his head, and the fool walketh in darkness: and yet I perceived that one event "As it happeneth to the fool, so will it happen even to me; and why was I then more wise?" Then said I in my heart, that this also is vanity. [16] For of the wise man, even as of the fool, there is no remembrance for ever; seeing that in the days to come all will have been long forgotten. And how doth the wise man die even as the fool! [17] So I hated life, because the work that is wrought under the sun was grievous unto me; for all is vanity and a striving after wind.

[18] And I hated all my labor wherein I labored under the sun, seeing that I must leave it unto the man that shall be after me. [19] And who knoweth whether he will be a wise man or a fool? yet will he have rule over all my labor wherein I have labored, and wherein I have showed myself wise under the sun. This also is vanity. [20] Therefore I turned about to cause my heart to despair concerning all the labor wherein I had labored under the sun. [21] For there is a man whose labor is with wisdom, and with knowledge, and with skilfulness; yet to a man that hath not labored therein shall he leave it for his portion. This also is vanity and a great evil. [22] For what hath a man of all his labor, and of the striving of his heart, wherein he laboreth under the sun? [23] For all his days are but sorrows, and his travail is grief; yea, even in the night his heart taketh no rest. This also is vanity.

[24] There is nothing better for a man than that he should eat and drink, and make his soul enjoy good in his labor. This also I saw, that it is from the hand of God. [25] For who can eat, or who can have enjoyment, more than I? [26] For to the man that pleaseth him, God giveth wisdom, and knowledge, and joy; but to the sinner he giveth travail, to gather and to heap up, that he may give to him that pleaseth God. This also is vanity and a striving after wind.

Bible Study Questions and Answers

1. Who wrote Ecclesiastes? What did he call himself?
   Solomon. He called himself the "Preacher."

2. What did Solomon say to himself in Ecclesiastes 1:2?
   Solomon refers to everything as vanity.

3. What was Solomon searching to find?
   He wanted to search and find wisdom regarding all things

4. List the things that Solomon did to accomplish his goal?
   Solomon built great houses, planted great gardens, bought men and women servants, had lard flocks, accumulated gold and silver, and had singers in his household.

5. Where did all the possessions put Solomon in the rank of wealth among men?
   Solomon was the wealthiest man ever during the time of Jerusalem.

6. What did Solomon deny himself?
   Solomon did not deny himself anything.

7. What was Solomon's ultimate conclusion?
   Apart from God, pleasures are vanity and evil.

8. According to Solomon, what comes to one who is not content?
   Those who are not content are given trials that come from gathering more and more.

QUESTION 15 ANSWERS:
WHAT MAKES US CONTENT?

Bible Study
Daniel 1:1-15

In the third year of the reign of Jehoiakim king of Judah came Nebuchadnezzar king of Babylon unto Jerusalem, and besieged it. ² And the Lord gave

Jehoiakim king of Judah into his hand, with part of the vessels of the house of God; and he carried them into the land of Shinar to the house of his god: and he brought the vessels into the treasure-house of his god. ³ And the king spake unto Ashpenaz the master of his eunuchs, that he should bring in certain of the children of Israel, even of the seed royal and of the nobles; ⁴ youths in whom was no blemish, but well-favored, and skilful in all wisdom, and endued with knowledge, and understanding science, and such as had ability to stand in the king's palace; and that he should teach them the learning and the tongue of the Chaldeans. ⁵ And the king appointed for them a daily portion of the king's dainties, and of the wine which he drank, and that they should be nourished three years; that at the end thereof they should stand before the king. ⁶ Now among these were, of the children of Judah, Daniel, Hananiah, Mishael, and Azariah. ⁷ And the prince of the eunuchs gave names unto them: unto Daniel he gave the name of Belteshazzar; and to Hananiah, of Shadrach; and to Mishael, Meshach; and to Azariah, of Abednego.

⁸ But Daniel purposed in his heart that he would not defile himself with the king's dainties, nor with the wine which he drank: therefore he requested of the prince of the eunuchs that he might not defile himself. ⁹ Now God made Daniel to find kindness and compassion in the sight of the prince of the eunuchs. ¹⁰ And the prince of the eunuchs said unto Daniel, "I fear my lord the king, who hath appointed your food and your drink: for why should he see your faces worse looking than the youths that are of your own age? so would ye endanger my head with the king." ¹¹ Then said Daniel to the steward whom the prince of the eunuchs had appointed over Daniel, Hananiah, Mishael, and Azariah: ¹² "Prove thy servants, I beseech thee, ten days; and let them give us pulse to eat, and water to drink. ¹³ Then let our countenances be looked upon before thee, and the countenance of the youths that eat of the king's dainties; and as thou seest, deal with thy servants."

¹⁴ So he hearkened unto them in this matter, and proved them ten days. ¹⁵ And at the end of ten days their countenances appeared fairer, and they were fatter in flesh, than all the youths that did eat of the king's dainties.

Bible Study Questions and Answers

1. During the time Daniel was written, who was King of Judah?
   King Jehoiakim

2. Who defeated King Jehoiakim?
   King Nebuchadnezzar

3. What was the Lord's part in the battle between the two kings?
   The Lord gave Jehoiakim over to Nebuchadnezzar.

4. Who are the four main characters of Daniel 1? Give both of their names.
   a. Daniel = Belteshazzar
   b. Hananiah = Shadrach
   c. Mishael = Meshach
   d. Azariah = Abednego

5. What were the characteristics of the four boys?
   a. From royal families and nobility
   b. Youths without blemish
   c. Good appearance
   d. Skillful in wisdom
   e. Endowed with knowledge
   f. Understanding of the learning
   g. Competent

6. How were the youths to be treated?
   a. There were to be taught the literature and language of the Chaldeans.
   b. They were given a daily portion of the king's food and wine.

7. What was Daniel's request?
   Daniel requested that they only be fed vegetables and water.

8. What was the result of Daniel's request after the 10-day period?
   The boys were better in appearance and fatter in flesh than all the other youths who ate the king's food.

9. **What does the story of Daniel reveal about contentment with what God provides us?***

> God will provide what we need. Daniel, Hananiah, Mishael, and Azariah were the best of Israelites' youth who were taken into the king's court for his service. They were provided the best of the king's food; however, they could not defile God and so decided to live off vegetables and water only. God was glorified in actions because after the 10-day trial, Daniel and the others looked better than those who ate the king's food. God will provide for us.

*Individual responses may vary.

QUESTION 16 ANSWERS: SHOULD WE BE CONTENT WITH THE MONEY THAT WE EARN?

Bible Study
1 Timothy 6

Let as many as are servants under the yoke count their own masters worthy of all honor, that the name of God and the doctrine be not blasphemed. ² And they that have believing masters, let them not despise them, because they are brethren; but let them serve them the rather, because they that partake of the benefit are believing and beloved. These things teach and exhort.

³ If any man teacheth a different doctrine, and consenteth not to sound words, even the words of our Lord Jesus Christ, and to the doctrine which is according to godliness; ⁴ he is puffed up, knowing nothing, but doting about questionings and disputes of words, whereof cometh envy, strife, railings, evil surmisings, ⁵ wranglings of men corrupted in mind and bereft of the truth, supposing that godliness is a way of gain. ⁶ But godliness with contentment is great gain: ⁷ for we brought nothing into the world, for neither can we carry anything out; ⁸ but having food and covering we shall be therewith content. ⁹ But they that are minded to be rich fall into a temptation and a snare and many foolish and hurtful lusts, such as drown men in destruction and perdition. ¹⁰ For the love of money is a root of all kinds of evil: which some reaching

after have been led astray from the faith, and have pierced themselves through with many sorrows.

[11] But thou, O man of God, flee these things; and follow after righteousness, godliness, faith, love, patience, meekness. [12] Fight the good fight of the faith, lay hold on the life eternal, whereunto thou wast called, and didst confess the good confession in the sight of many witnesses. [13] I charge thee in the sight of God, who giveth life to all things, and of Christ Jesus, who before Pontius Pilate witnessed the good confession; [14] that thou keep the commandment, without spot, without reproach, until the appearing of our Lord Jesus Christ: [15] which in its own times he shall show, who is the blessed and only Potentate, the King of kings, and Lord of lords; [16] who only hath immortality, dwelling in light unapproachable; whom no man hath seen, nor can see: to whom be honor and power eternal. Amen.

[17] Charge them that are rich in this present world, that they be not high-minded, nor have their hope set on the uncertainty of riches, but on God, who giveth us richly all things to enjoy; [18] that they do good, that they be rich in good works, that they be ready to distribute, willing to communicate; [19] laying up in store for themselves a good foundation against the time to come, that they may lay hold on the life which is life indeed.

[20] O Timothy, guard that which is committed unto thee, turning away from the profane babblings and oppositions of the knowledge which is falsely so called; [21] which some professing have erred concerning the faith.

Grace be with you.

Bible Study Questions and Answers

1. What does Paul say about who that seek to constantly make more money?

They fall into temptation, into a snare, into many senseless and harmful desires that plunge people into ruin and destruction.

2. What does Paul say is the root of all kinds of evil?

Paul says that the love of money is the root of all kinds of evil.

3. What does Paul's saying mean to us?*

Money itself is nothing more than a tool to be used in exchange for other things. It is the love of money that is the root of all kinds of evil. The desire to have more money is so that we can exchange for more stuff.

4. What happens if we fall into a desire to want more?

Those who want or desire more can wander from their faith in Christ as savior and all-sufficient provider.

5. What is Paul's advice?

Paul's advice is to get away, to "flee" desires that cause us to wander from the Lord and, instead, we are to pursue such things as righteousness, gentleness, godliness, love, and faith.

6. Why do you believe Paul asks us to flee the pursuit of desiring more money?*

Paul is genuinely concerned for the church and doesn't want us to put our faith in Christ in jeopardy and begin to rely on ourselves. We must always remember that God is our lone provider.

*Individual responses may vary.

OUR FINANCIAL FAITHFULNESS

QUESTION 17 ANSWERS: CAN GOD USE GIVING TO TEST OUR FAITHFULNESS IN HIM?

Bible Study
Genesis 22

And it came to pass after these things, that God did prove Abraham, and said unto him, Abraham; and he said, "Here am I." [2] And he said, "Take now thy son, thine only son, whom thou lovest, even Isaac, and get thee into the land of Moriah; and offer him there for a burnt offering upon one of the mountains which I will tell thee of." [3] And Abraham rose early in the morning, and saddled his ass, and took two of his young men with him, and Isaac his son; and he clave the wood for the burnt offering, and rose up, and went unto the place of which God had told him. [4] On the third day Abraham lifted up his eyes, and saw the place afar off. [5] And Abraham said unto his young men, "Abide ye here with the ass, and I and the lad will go yonder; and we will worship, and come again to you." [6] And Abraham took the wood of the burnt offering, and laid it upon Isaac his son; and he took in his hand the fire and the knife; and they went both of them together. [7] And Isaac spake unto Abraham his father, and said, "My father." and he said, "Here am I, my son." And he said, "Behold, the fire and the wood: but where is the lamb for a burnt offering?" [8] And Abraham said, "God will provide himself the lamb for a burnt offering, my son," so they went both of them together.

[9] And they came to the place which God had told him of; and Abraham built the altar there, and laid the wood in order, and bound Isaac his son, and laid him on the altar, upon the wood. [10] And Abraham stretched forth his hand, and took the knife to slay his son. [11] And the angel of Jehovah called unto him out of heaven, and said, "Abraham, Abraham," and he said, "Here am I." [12] And he said, "Lay not thy hand upon the lad, neither do thou anything unto him; for now I know that thou fearest God, seeing thou hast not withheld thy son, thine only son, from me." [13] And Abraham lifted up his eyes, and looked,

and, behold, behind him a ram caught in the thicket by his horns: and Abraham went and took the ram, and offered him up for a burnt offering in the stead of his son. [14] And Abraham called the name of that place Jehovah-Jireh: as it is said to this day, In the mount of Jehovah it shall be provided. [15] And the angel of Jehovah called unto Abraham a second time out of heaven, [16] and said, "By myself have I sworn, saith Jehovah, because thou hast done this thing, and hast not withheld thy son, thine only son, [17] that in blessing I will bless thee, and in multiplying I will multiply thy seed as the stars of the heavens, and as the sand which is upon the seashore; and thy seed shall possess the gate of his enemies; [18] and in thy seed shall all the nations of the earth be blessed; because thou hast obeyed my voice." [19] So Abraham returned unto his young men, and they rose up and went together to Beersheba; and Abraham dwelt at Beersheba.

Bible Study Questions and Answers

1. What did God later do to Abraham?
   God tested Abraham.

2. What did God ask Abraham to do?
   God asked Abraham to sacrifice his only son Isaac.

3. Why would God's request be considered a test of Abraham's faithfulness?*
   Isaac was Abraham's only son and God had promised Abraham many nations. Abraham loved Isaac dearly.

4. How does Abraham's response relate to giving?
   Abraham was willing to "give up" Isaac because he had faith in God and that is what God commanded.

5. After reading the story of Abraham and Isaac, what are you willing to give up?*
   This is a great opportunity for us to reflect and consider what we are willing to give up in the name of Christ.

*Individual responses may vary.

QUESTION 19 ANSWERS:
WHY DO WE GIVE TO OUR NEIGHBOR?

Bible Study
Deuteronomy 15:1–15

At the end of every seven years thou shalt make a release. ² And this is the manner of the release: every creditor shall release that which he hath lent unto his neighbor; he shall not exact it of his neighbor and his brother; because Jehovah's release hath been proclaimed. ³ Of a foreigner thou mayest exact it: but whatsoever of thine is with thy brother thy hand shall release. ⁴ Howbeit there shall be no poor with thee (for Jehovah will surely bless thee in the land which Jehovah thy God giveth thee for an inheritance to possess it), ⁵ if only thou diligently hearken unto the voice of Jehovah thy God, to observe to do all this commandment which I command thee this day. ⁶ For Jehovah thy God will bless thee, as he promised thee: and thou shalt lend unto many nations, but thou shalt not borrow; and thou shalt rule over many nations, but they shall not rule over thee.

⁷ If there be with thee a poor man, one of thy brethren, within any of thy gates in thy land which Jehovah thy God giveth thee, thou shalt not harden thy heart, nor shut thy hand from thy poor brother; ⁸ but thou shalt surely open thy hand unto him, and shalt surely lend him sufficient for his need in that which he wanteth. ⁹ Beware that there be not a base thought in thy heart, saying, The seventh year, the year of release, is at hand; and thine eye be evil against thy poor brother, and thou give him nought; and he cry unto Jehovah against thee, and it be sin unto thee. ¹⁰ Thou shalt surely give him, and thy heart shall not be grieved when thou givest unto him; because that for this thing Jehovah thy God will bless thee in all thy work, and in all that thou puttest thy hand unto. ¹¹ For the poor will never cease out of the land: therefore I command thee, saying, Thou shalt surely open thy hand unto thy brother, to thy needy, and to thy poor, in thy land.

¹² If thy brother, a Hebrew man, or a Hebrew woman, be sold unto thee, and serve thee six years; then in the seventh year thou shalt let him go free from thee. ¹³ And when thou lettest him go free from thee, thou shalt not let him

go empty: ¹⁴ thou shalt furnish him liberally out of thy flock, and out of thy threshing-floor, and out of thy winepress; as Jehovah thy God hath blessed thee thou shalt give unto him. ¹⁵ And thou shalt remember that thou wast a bondman in the land of Egypt, and Jehovah thy God redeemed thee: therefore I command thee this thing today.

Bible Study Questions and Answers

1. What is the first thing we shouldn't do when seeing a poor brother?

   When faced with seeing a brother in need, we are not to become stingy or proud.

2. What then shall we do when seeing a poor brother?

   We are to be willing to give him what he needs, whatever that may be.

3. How is Deuteronomy 15:9 to be interpreted?

   In the Israelite community, at the end of every seven years, any outstanding debts owed were wiped clean because the Lord's release was proclaimed (v. 2). So, if the seventh year (the year for cancelling debts) was approaching, an Israelite might be hesitant to lend to a brother because of the likelihood of not getting paid back. But God said that if a loan was withheld and the Hebrew brother cried out to him, then the person withholding the loan would be guilty of sin.

4. What will the Lord do if we give freely and without grudging in our hearts?

   God indicates that he will bless us in all we do.

5. Why was the practice of cancelling debts every seven years established by God?

   God established the practice of the forgiveness of debt because there will always be poor people in the land. The practice also served as a foreshadow of the time of Christ when a new institution would be given—the *"forgiveness of our debts as we forgive the debts of others"* (Matt. 6:14-15).

6. What was the process if a fellow Hebrew was sold to a Hebrew master?

A Hebrew man or woman sold into slavery was to serve the Hebrew master for six years and then, in the seventh year, be set free. And when set free, they were to be furnished liberally from the master's livestock, grains, wine and oil.

7. Why were the Hebrew masters commanded to give liberally from their livestock and storehouses?

The purpose of giving liberally to a newly-released Hebrew slave was to glorify God in remembrance of his blessing when all the Hebrews were redeemed from the land of Egypt, freed from slavery and bestowed with great wealth from the Egyptians.

QUESTION 20 ANSWERS:
WHAT DOES GIVING PROVE TO US?

Bible Study
Galatians 5

For freedom did Christ set us free: stand fast therefore, and be not entangled again in a yoke of bondage.

[2] Behold, I Paul say unto you, that, if ye receive circumcision, Christ will profit you nothing. [3] Yea, I testify again to every man that receiveth circumcision, that he is a debtor to do the whole law. [4] Ye are severed from Christ, ye who would be justified by the law; ye are fallen away from grace. [5] For we through the Spirit by faith wait for the hope of righteousness. [6] For in Christ Jesus neither circumcision availeth anything, nor uncircumcision; but faith working through love. [7] Ye were running well; who hindered you that ye should not obey the truth? [8] This persuasion came not of him that calleth you. [9] A little leaven leaveneth the whole lump. [10] I have confidence to you-ward in the Lord, that ye will be none otherwise minded: but he that troubleth you shall bear his judgment, whosoever he be. [11] But I, brethren, if I still preach circumcision, why am I still persecuted? then hath the stumbling-block of the cross

been done away. ¹² I would that they that unsettle you would even go beyond circumcision.

¹³ For ye, brethren, were called for freedom; only use not your freedom for an occasion to the flesh, but through love be servants one to another. ¹⁴ For the whole law is fulfilled in one word, even in this: Thou shalt love thy neighbor as thyself. ¹⁵ But if ye bite and devour one another, take heed that ye be not consumed one of another.

¹⁶ But I say, Walk by the Spirit, and ye shall not fulfil the lust of the flesh. ¹⁷ For the flesh lusteth against the Spirit, and the Spirit against the flesh; for these are contrary the one to the other; that ye may not do the things that ye would. ¹⁸ But if ye are led by the Spirit, ye are not under the law. ¹⁹ Now the works of the flesh are manifest, which are these: fornication, uncleanness, lasciviousness, ²⁰ idolatry, sorcery, enmities, strife, jealousies, wraths, factions, divisions, parties, ²¹ envyings, drunkenness, revellings, and such like; of which I forewarn you, even as I did forewarn you, that they who practise such things shall not inherit the kingdom of God. ²² But the fruit of the Spirit is love, joy, peace, longsuffering, kindness, goodness, faithfulness, ²³ meekness, self-control; against such there is no law. ²⁴ And they that are of Christ Jesus have crucified the flesh with the passions and the lusts thereof.

²⁵ If we live by the Spirit, by the Spirit let us also walk. ²⁶ Let us not become vainglorious, provoking one another, envying one another.

Bible Study Questions and Answers

1. How does giving to our neighbor reveal *love* in us?*
   One of the most basic ways we show our love for someone is by giving. We can give our time, our resources, and our skills to demonstrate what they mean to us.

2. How does giving to our neighbor reveal joy in us?*
   The act of giving should elicit joy in our lives, something provided by the Holy Spirit. In most cases, when we give, we generally feel very good.

3. How does giving to our neighbor reveal *peace* in us?*

When we give to our neighbor, we are giving up something and the act of giving demonstrates a level of peace when accepting what we already have. This can be a sign of true contentment.

4. How does giving to our neighbor reveal *patience* in us?*

When we give to our neighbor, we are giving up something that could otherwise remain our own; patience is demonstrated by us when rightly awaiting the ability to earn back the money we gave away.

5. How does giving to our neighbor reveal *kindness* in us?*

When we give to our neighbor, we are showing kindness to them and offering something to them that they may need.

6. How does giving to our neighbor reveal *goodness* in us?*

When we give to our neighbor, we are following the pattern of Christ who is our example of goodness.

7. How does giving to our neighbor reveal *faithfulness* in us?*

When we give to our neighbor, we must be faithful that the Lord will continue to provide for our own needs.

8. How does giving to our neighbor reveal *gentleness* in us?*

Gentleness is a posture of humility. When we give to our neighbor, we desire to help them meet a need, but we do so with an attitude of humility and out of a true concern for their wellbeing.

9. How does giving to our neighbor reveal *self-control* in us?*

Although it may seem obvious, when we give to our neighbor, we are controlling our own desires for the things we want. When we give, we are giving up our immediate desires for the benefit of others.

*Individual responses may vary.

GOD'S PERSPECTIVE ON GIVING

QUESTION 21 ANSWERS:
WHAT IS GOD'S ATTITUDE TOWARD GIVING?

Bible Study
Genesis 1

In the beginning God created the heavens and the earth. [2] And the earth was waste and void; and darkness was upon the face of the deep: and the Spirit of God moved upon the face of the waters. [3] And God said, "Let there be light": and there was light. [4] And God saw the light, that it was good: and God divided the light from the darkness. [5] And God called the light Day, and the darkness he called Night. And there was evening and there was morning, one day.

[6] And God said, "Let there be a firmament in the midst of the waters, and let it divide the waters from the waters." [7] And God made the firmament, and divided the waters which were under the firmament from the waters which were above the firmament: and it was so. [8] And God called the firmament Heaven. And there was evening and there was morning, a second day.

[9] And God said, "Let the waters under the heavens be gathered together unto one place, and let the dry land appear," and it was so. [10] And God called the dry land Earth; and the gathering together of the waters called he Seas: and God saw that it was good. [11] And God said, "Let the earth put forth grass, herbs yielding seed, and fruit-trees bearing fruit after their kind, wherein is the seed thereof, upon the earth," and it was so. [12] And the earth brought forth grass, herbs yielding seed after their kind, and trees bearing fruit, wherein is the seed thereof, after their kind, and God saw that it was good. [13] And there was evening and there was morning, a third day.

[14] And God said, "Let there be lights in the firmament of heaven to divide the day from the night; and let them be for signs, and for seasons, and for days and years, [15] and let them be for lights in the firmament of heaven to give light upon the earth," and it was so. [16] And God made the two great lights; the greater light to rule the day, and the lesser light to rule the night: he made the

stars also. [17] And God set them in the firmament of heaven to give light upon the earth, [18] and to rule over the day and over the night, and to divide the light from the darkness: and God saw that it was good. [19] And there was evening and there was morning, a fourth day.

[20] And God said, "Let the waters swarm with swarms of living creatures, and let birds fly above the earth in the open firmament of heaven." [21] And God created the great sea-monsters, and every living creature that moveth, where-with the waters swarmed, after their kind, and every winged bird after its kind, and God saw that it was good. [22] And God blessed them, saying, "Be fruitful, and multiply, and fill the waters in the seas, and let birds multiply on the earth." [23] And there was evening and there was morning, a fifth day.

[24] And God said, "Let the earth bring forth living creatures after their kind, cattle, and creeping things, and beasts of the earth after their kind," and it was so. [25] And God made the beasts of the earth after their kind, and the cattle after their kind, and everything that creepeth upon the ground after its kind, and God saw that it was good. [26] And God said, "Let us make man in our image, after our likeness: and let them have dominion over the fish of the sea, and over the birds of the heavens, and over the cattle, and over all the earth, and over every creeping thing that creepeth upon the earth." [27] And God created man in his own image, in the image of God created he him; male and female created he them. [28] And God blessed them: and God said unto them, "Be fruitful, and multiply, and replenish the earth, and subdue it; and have dominion over the fish of the sea, and over the birds of the heavens, and over every living thing that moveth upon the earth." [29] And God said, "Behold, I have given you every herb yielding seed, which is upon the face of all the earth, and every tree, in which is the fruit of a tree yielding seed; to you it shall be for food; [30] and to every beast of the earth, and to every bird of the heavens, and to everything that creepeth upon the earth, wherein there is life, I have given every green herb for food," and it was so. [31] And God saw everything that he had made, and, behold, it was very good. And there was evening and there was morning, the sixth day.

Bible Study Questions and Answers

1. What did God give us on the *first* day?
   God gave us light.

2. What did God give us on the *second* day?
   God made the heavens.

3. What did God give us on the *third* day?
   God gave us land and seas, and plants that reproduce.

4. What did God give us on the *fourth* day?
   God made the sun, moon, and stars.

5. What did God give us on the *fifth* day?
   God made the animals that live in the water and the animals that fly in the heavens.

6. What did God gives us on the *sixth* day?
   God made us in his image, after his likeness.

7. What was the ultimate gift that God gave to his creation?*
   God gave his only son, Jesus Christ!

Individual responses may vary.

QUESTION 22 ANSWERS:
WHAT IS TO BE OUR ATTITUDE TOWARD GIVING?

Bible Study
1 Chronicles 29

And David the king said unto all the assembly, "Solomon my son, whom alone God hath chosen, is yet young and tender, and the work is great; for the palace is not for man, but for Jehovah God. ² Now I have prepared with all my might for the house of my God the gold for the things of gold, and the silver for the things of silver, and the brass for the things of brass, the iron for the things of iron, and wood for the things of wood; onyx stones, and stones to be set, stones for inlaid work, and of divers colors, and all manner of precious stones, and marble stones in abundance. ³ Moreover also, because I have set my affection on the house of my God, seeing that I have a treasure of mine own of gold and silver, I give it unto the house of my God, over and above all that I have prepared for the holy house, ⁴ even three thousand talents of gold, of the gold of Ophir, and seven thousand talents of refined silver, wherewith to overlay the walls of the houses; ⁵ of gold for the things of gold, and of silver for the things of silver, and for all manner of work to be made by the hands of artificers. Who then offereth willingly to consecrate himself this day unto Jehovah?"

⁶ Then the princes of the fathers' houses, and the princes of the tribes of Israel, and the captains of thousands and of hundreds, with the rulers over the king's work, offered willingly; ⁷ and they gave for the service of the house of God of gold five thousand talents and ten thousand darics, and of silver ten thousand talents, and of brass eighteen thousand talents, and of iron a hundred thousand talents. ⁸ And they with whom precious stones were found gave them to the treasure of the house of Jehovah, under the hand of Jehiel the Gershonite. ⁹ Then the people rejoiced, for that they offered willingly, because with a perfect heart they offered willingly to Jehovah: and David the king also rejoiced with great joy.

¹⁰ Wherefore David blessed Jehovah before all the assembly; and David said, "Blessed be thou, O Jehovah, the God of Israel our father, for ever and ever. ¹¹ Thine, O Jehovah, is the greatness, and the power, and the glory, and the victory, and the majesty: for all that is in the heavens and in the earth is thine; thine is the kingdom, O Jehovah, and thou art exalted as head above all. ¹² Both riches and honor come of thee, and thou rulest over all; and in thy hand is power and might; and in thy hand it is to make great, and to give strength unto all. ¹³ Now therefore, our God, we thank thee, and praise thy glorious name. ¹⁴ But who am I, and what is my people, that we should be able to offer so willingly after this sort? for all things come of thee, and of thine own have we given thee. ¹⁵ For we are strangers before thee, and sojourners, as all our fathers were: our days on the earth are as a shadow, and there is no abiding. ¹⁶ O Jehovah our God, all this store that we have prepared to build thee a house for thy holy name cometh of thy hand, and is all thine own. ¹⁷ I know also, my God, that thou triest the heart, and hast pleasure in uprightness. As for me, in the uprightness of my heart I have willingly offered all these things: and now have I seen with joy thy people, that are present here, offer willingly unto thee.

[18] O Jehovah, the God of Abraham, of Isaac, and of Israel, our fathers, keep this for ever in the imagination of the thoughts of the heart of thy people, and prepare their heart unto thee; [19] and give unto Solomon my son a perfect heart, to keep thy commandments, thy testimonies, and thy statutes, and to do all these things, and to build the palace, for which I have made provision."

[20] And David said to all the assembly, "Now bless Jehovah your God." And all the assembly blessed Jehovah, the God of their fathers, and bowed down their heads, and worshipped Jehovah, and the king. [21] And they sacrificed sacrifices unto Jehovah, and offered burnt offerings unto Jehovah, on the morrow after that day, even a thousand bullocks, a thousand rams, and a thousand lambs, with their drink-offerings, and sacrifices in abundance for all Israel, [22] and did eat and drink before Jehovah on that day with great gladness.

And they made Solomon the son of David king the second time, and anointed him unto Jehovah to be prince, and Zadok to be priest. [23] Then Solomon sat on the throne of Jehovah as king instead of David his father, and prospered; and all Israel obeyed him. [24] And all the princes, and the mighty men, and all the sons likewise of king David, submitted themselves unto Solomon the king. [25] And Jehovah magnified Solomon exceedingly in the sight of all Israel, and bestowed upon him such royal majesty as had not been on any king before him in Israel.

[26] Now David the son of Jesse reigned over all Israel. [27] And the time that he reigned over Israel was forty years; seven years reigned he in Hebron, and thirty and three years reigned he in Jerusalem. [28] And he died in a good old age, full of days, riches, and honor: and Solomon his son reigned in his stead. [29] Now the acts of David the king, first and last, behold, they are written in the history of Samuel the seer, and in the history of Nathan the prophet, and in the history of Gad the seer, [30] with all his reign and his might, and the times that went over him, and over Israel, and over all the kingdoms of the countries.

Bible Study Questions and Answers

1. What is taking place in this passage?

   David is talking to the assembly of Israelites and telling them about the upcoming building of the temple.

2. Who is responsible for building the temple?
   King David's son, Solomon

3. What did David tell the Israelites about what he had done as king?
   During his reign, and in preparation for building the holy temple, King Davad amassed large quantities of gold, silver, bronze, iron, wood, and precious stones.

4. What did David personally provide for building the temple? And, why?
   David gave gold and silver out of his personal treasury to build the temple. He did so because of his devotion to the house of God.

5. What did David ask of those in attendance?
   Who then will give an offering willingly, consecrating himself to the Lord today?

6. In your own words, what was David asking?*
   David was preaching an evangelistic message: he first publicly recognized that all of the possessions that he and the people were providing for the building of the holy temple were already God's (they were merely giving back to God what he had entrusted to them), and David wanted his people to experience a devotion to God as he had experienced. Why? Because David knew that from out of this devotion and love comes acts of generosity.

*Individual responses may vary.

QUESTION 23 ANSWERS:
WHAT DOES A GOOD ATTITUDE IN GIVING BRING?

Bible Study

Romans 15

Now we that are strong ought to bear the infirmities of the weak, and not to please ourselves. ² Let each one of us please his neighbor for that which is good, unto edifying. ³ For Christ also pleased not himself; but, as it is written, "The reproaches of them that reproached thee fell upon me." ⁴ For whatsoever things were written aforetime were written for our learning, that through patience and through comfort of the Scriptures we might have hope. ⁵ Now the God of patience and of comfort grant you to be of the same mind one with another according to Christ Jesus: ⁶ that with one accord ye may with one mouth glorify the God and Father of our Lord Jesus Christ. ⁷ Wherefore receive ye one another, even as Christ also received you, to the glory of God. ⁸ For I say that Christ hath been made a minister of the circumcision for the truth of God, that he might confirm the promises given unto the fathers, ⁹ and that the Gentiles might glorify God for his mercy; as it is written,

"Therefore will I give praise unto thee among the Gentiles,
And sing unto thy name."
¹⁰ And again he saith,
"Rejoice, ye Gentiles, with his people."
¹¹ And again,
"Praise the Lord, all ye Gentiles;
And let all the peoples praise him."
¹² And again, Isaiah saith,
"There shall be the root of Jesse,
And he that ariseth to rule over the Gentiles;
On him shall the Gentiles hope."
¹³ Now the God of hope fill you with all joy and peace in believing, that ye
may abound in hope, in the power of the Holy Spirit.

¹⁴ And I myself also am persuaded of you, my brethren, that ye yourselves are full of goodness, filled with all knowledge, able also to admonish one another. ¹⁵ But I write the more boldly unto you in some measure, as putting you again in remembrance, because of the grace that was given me of God, ¹⁶ that I should be a minister of Christ Jesus unto the Gentiles, ministering the gospel of God, that the offering up of the Gentiles might be made acceptable, being sanctified by the Holy Spirit. ¹⁷ I have therefore my glorying in Christ Jesus in things pertaining to God. ¹⁸ For I will not dare to speak of any things save those which Christ wrought through me, for the obedience of the Gentiles, by word and deed, ¹⁹ in the power of signs and wonders, in the power of the

Holy Spirit; so that from Jerusalem, and round about even unto Illyricum, I have fully preached the gospel of Christ; [20] yea, making it my aim so to preach the gospel, not where Christ was already named, that I might not build upon another man's foundation; [21] but, as it is written,

> "They shall see, to whom no tidings of him came,
> And they who have not heard shall understand."

[22] Wherefore also I was hindered these many times from coming to you: [23] but now, having no more any place in these regions, and having these many years a longing to come unto you, [24] whensoever I go unto Spain (for I hope to see you in my journey, and to be brought on my way thitherward by you, if first in some measure I shall have been satisfied with your company)— [25] but now, I say, I go unto Jerusalem, ministering unto the saints. [26] For it hath been the good pleasure of Macedonia and Achaia to make a certain contribution for the poor among the saints that are at Jerusalem. [27] Yea, it hath been their good pleasure; and their debtors they are. For if the Gentiles have been made partakers of their spiritual things, they owe it to them also to minister unto them in carnal things. [28] When therefore I have accomplished this, and have sealed to them this fruit, I will go on by you unto Spain. [29] And I know that, when I come unto you, I shall come in the fulness of the blessing of Christ.

[30] Now I beseech you, brethren, by our Lord Jesus Christ, and by the love of the Spirit, that ye strive together with me in your prayers to God for me; [31] that I may be delivered from them that are disobedient in Judaea, and that my ministration which I have for Jerusalem may be acceptable to the saints; [32] that I may come unto you in joy through the will of God, and together with you find rest. [33] Now the God of peace be with you all. Amen.

Bible Study Questions and Answers

1. What does Paul say is the obligation of the strong?
   The obligation for those of us who are strong is to bear with the failings of the weak and not to please ourselves.

2. What brings us hope?

Paul shares that the Scriptures are a source of learning, comfort and hope, but the ultimate source of hope for Gentiles is the root of Jesse—Christ Jesus.

3. What is Paul's request? And, how are we to do it?

Paul's request is that we should live in harmony with one another, in accord with Christ Jesus, and that together we may with one voice glorify the God and Father of our Lord Jesus Christ. We can live in one accord when we welcome one another as Christ has welcomed us, for the glory of God.

4. Reflect on Romans 15:13. How does hope, joy, peace in believing, and community relate to our giving?*

We give knowing that we have hope in Christ (who became a servant to the circumcised to show God's truthfulness), which gives us joy to know we are part of God's kingdom, and we can be in community by helping others when they are weak.

* Individual responses may vary.

ATTITUDE OF GIVING

QUESTION 25 ANSWERS:
SHOULD GIVING BECOME OUR PRIMARY FOCUS?

Bible Study
1 Chronicles 16 and Acts 13:23

1 Chronicles 16

And they brought in the ark of God, and set it in the midst of the tent that David had pitched for it: and they offered burnt offerings and peace-offerings before God. ² And when David had made an end of offering the burnt offering and the peace-offerings, he blessed the people in the name of Jehovah. ³ And he dealt to every one of Israel, both man and woman, to every one a loaf of bread, and a portion of flesh, and a cake of raisins.

⁴ And he appointed certain of the Levites to minister before the ark of Jehovah, and to celebrate and to thank and praise Jehovah, the God of Israel: ⁵ Asaph the chief, and second to him Zechariah, Jeiel, and Shemiramoth, and Jehiel, and Mattithiah, and Eliab, and Benaiah, and Obed-edom, and Jeiel, with psalteries and with harps; and Asaph with cymbals, sounding aloud; ⁶ and Benaiah and Jahaziel the priests with trumpets continually, before the ark of the covenant of God.

⁷ Then on that day did David first ordain to give thanks unto Jehovah, by the hand of Asaph and his brethren.

> ⁸ *O give thanks unto Jehovah, call upon his name;*
> *Make known his doings among the peoples.*
> ⁹ *Sing unto him, sing praises unto him;*
> *Talk ye of all his marvellous works.*
> ¹⁰ *Glory ye in his holy name;*
> *Let the heart of them rejoice that seek Jehovah.*
> ¹¹ *Seek ye Jehovah and his strength;*
> *Seek his face evermore.*
> ¹² *Remember his marvellous works that he hath done,*
> *His wonders, and the judgments of his mouth,*
> ¹³ *O ye seed of Israel his servant,*
> *Ye children of Jacob, his chosen ones.*

[14] *He is Jehovah our God;*
His judgments are in all the earth.
[15] *Remember his covenant for ever,*
The word which he commanded to a thousand generations,
[16] *The covenant which he made with Abraham,*
And his oath unto Isaac,
[17] *And confirmed the same unto Jacob for a statute,*
To Israel for an everlasting covenant,
[18] *Saying, "Unto thee will I give the land of Canaan,*
The lot of your inheritance."
[19] *When ye were but a few men in number,*
Yea, very few, and sojourners in it;
[20] *And they went about from nation to nation,*
And from one kingdom to another people.
[21] *He suffered no man to do them wrong;*
Yea, he reproved kings for their sakes,
[22] *Saying, "Touch not mine anointed ones,*
And do my prophets no harm."
[23] *Sing unto Jehovah, all the earth;*
Show forth his salvation from day to day.
[24] *Declare his glory among the nations,*
His marvellous works among all the peoples.
[25] *For great is Jehovah, and greatly to be praised:*
He also is to be feared above all gods.
[26] *For all the gods of the peoples are idols:*
But Jehovah made the heavens.
[27] *Honor and majesty are before him:*
Strength and gladness are in his place.
[28] *Ascribe unto Jehovah, ye kindreds of the peoples,*
Ascribe unto Jehovah glory and strength;
[29] *Ascribe unto Jehovah the glory due unto his name:*
Bring an offering, and come before him:
Worship Jehovah in holy array.
[30] *Tremble before him, all the earth:*
The world also is established that it cannot be moved.

³¹ Let the heavens be glad, and let the earth rejoice;
And let them say among the nations, "Jehovah reigneth."
³² Let the sea roar, and the fulness thereof;
Let the field exult, and all that is therein;
³³ Then shall the trees of the wood sing for joy before Jehovah;
For he cometh to judge the earth.
³⁴ O give thanks unto Jehovah; for he is good;
For his lovingkindness endureth for ever.
³⁵ And say ye, "Save us, O God of our salvation,
And gather us together and deliver us from the nations,
To give thanks unto thy holy name,
And to triumph in thy praise."
³⁶ Blessed be Jehovah, the God of Israel,
From everlasting even to everlasting.
And all the people said, "Amen," and praised Jehovah.

³⁷ So he left there, before the ark of the covenant of Jehovah, Asaph and his brethren, to minister before the ark continually, as every day's work required; ³⁸ and Obed-edom with their brethren, threescore and eight; Obed-edom also the son of Jeduthun and Hosah to be doorkeepers; ³⁹ and Zadok the priest, and his brethren the priests, before the tabernacle of Jehovah in the high place that was at Gibeon, ⁴⁰ to offer burnt offerings unto Jehovah upon the altar of burnt offering continually morning and evening, even according to all that is written in the law of Jehovah, which he commanded unto Israel; ⁴¹ and with them Heman and Jeduthun, and the rest that were chosen, who were mentioned by name, to give thanks to Jehovah, because his" lovingkindness endureth forever"; ⁴² and with them Heman and Jeduthun with trumpets and cymbals for those that should sound aloud, and with instruments for the songs of God; and the sons of Jeduthun to be at the gate. ⁴³ And all the people departed every man to his house: and David returned to bless his house.

Acts 13:23

"From this man's descendants God has brought to Israel the Savior Jesus, as he promised."

Bible Study Questions and Answers

1. **What event was being celebrated by the Israelites?**
   The Ark of the Covenant was being placed in the tabernacle.

2. **During this time of celebration, how does David start his speech?**
   David starts his speech by
   a. giving thanks to the Lord.
   b. galling upon the Lord's name.
   c. making known his deeds among the peoples.
   d. singing praises to him.
   e. telling of his wondrous works.
   f. claiming that those who seek the Lord rejoice.
   g. seeking the Lord and his strength (continually).
   h. remembering the Lord's works, his miracles, and his judgments.

3. **What is David asking of the Israelites?**
   David was remembering what God had done:
   a. He is the Lord, the one true God.
   b. His judgments are in all the earth.
   c. God made covenants with Abraham, Isaac, and Jacob.
   d. The Lord gave Canaan.
   e. The Lord provided protection.

4. **What was the focus of the last part of David's song?**
   David's focus in the last part of his song was to
   a. sing to the Lord.
   b. tell of his Salvation.
   c. declare his glory.
   d. tell of his marvelous works.
   e. acknowledge that the Lord is to be feared above all gods.
   f. assert that the gods of the people are worthless.
   g. declare the Lord's splendor and majesty.

5. **Why did God select David as king?**
   God found favor in David, who was the son of Jesse. God knew that David would be faithful to do his will.

6. How does David's story connect to the answer that our primary purpose is to glorify God?*

David was selected as King because his heart was pointed toward God and would do anything the Lord wanted, no questions asked. David was selected to be anointed king when he was still a shepherd boy, not one who was in the temple giving. God desired one that willingly would do all the Lord required.

Individual responses may vary.

QUESTION 26 ANSWERS:
WHAT DOES GOD'S WORD SAY ABOUT OUR REWARD FOR GIVING?

Bible Study
John 14:1–12 and 1 Corinthians 2

John 14:1–12

"Let not your heart be troubled: believe in God, believe also in me. ^{2} In my Father's house are many mansions; if it were not so, I would have told you; for I go to prepare a place for you. ^{3} And if I go and prepare a place for you, I come again, and will receive you unto myself; that where I am, there ye may be also. ^{4} And whither I go, ye know the way." ^{5} Thomas saith unto him, "Lord, we know not whither thou goest; how know we the way?" ^{6} Jesus saith unto him, "I am the way, and the truth, and the life: no one cometh unto the Father, but by me. ^{7} If ye had known me, ye would have known my Father also: from henceforth ye know him, and have seen him." ^{8} Philip saith unto him, "Lord, show us the Father, and it sufficeth us." ^{9} Jesus saith unto him, "Have I been so long time with you, and dost thou not know me, Philip? he that hath seen me hath seen the Father; how sayest thou, 'Show us the Father'? ^{10} Believest thou not that I am in the Father, and the Father in me? the words that I say unto you I speak not from myself: but the Father abiding in me doeth his works. ^{11} Believe me that I am in the Father, and the Father in me: or else believe me for the very works' sake. ^{12} Verily, verily, I say unto you, He that believeth on me, the works that I do shall he do also; and greater works than these shall he do; because I go unto the Father."

1 Corinthians 2

And I, brethren, when I came unto you, came not with excellency of speech or of wisdom, proclaiming to you the testimony of God. ² For I determined not to know anything among you, save Jesus Christ, and him crucified. ³ And I was with you in weakness, and in fear, and in much trembling. ⁴ And my speech and my preaching were not in persuasive words of wisdom, but in demonstration of the Spirit and of power: ⁵ that your faith should not stand in the wisdom of men, but in the power of God.⁶ We speak wisdom, however, among them that are fullgrown: yet a wisdom not of this world, nor of the rulers of this world, who are coming to nought: ⁷ but we speak God's wisdom in a mystery, even the wisdom that hath been hidden, which God foreordained before the worlds unto our glory: ⁸ which none of the rulers of this world hath known: for had they known it, they would not have crucified the Lord of glory: ⁹ but as it is written,

> *"Things which eye saw not, and ear heard not,*
> *And which entered not into the heart of man,*
> *Whatsoever things God prepared for them that love him."*

¹⁰ But unto us God revealed them through the Spirit: for the Spirit searcheth all things, yea, the deep things of God. ¹¹ For who among men knoweth the things of a man, save the spirit of the man, which is in him? even so the things of God none knoweth, save the Spirit of God. ¹² But we received, not the spirit of the world, but the spirit which is from God; that we might know the things that were freely given to us of God. ¹³ Which things also we speak, not in words which man's wisdom teacheth, but which the Spirit teacher combining spiritual things with spiritual words. ¹⁴ Now the natural man receiveth not the things of the Spirit of God: for they are foolishness unto him; and he cannot know them, because they are spiritually judged. ¹⁵ But he that is spiritual judgeth all things, and he himself is judged of no man. ¹⁶ "For who hath known the mind of the Lord, that he should instruct him?" But we have the mind of Christ.

Bible Study Questions and Answers

1. What does Jesus say to his disciples to comfort them?
   a. "Do not be troubled."
   b. "Believe in God."
   c. "Believe also in me."

2. Where was Jesus getting ready to go? And, what did Jesus say he would do next?

   Jesus was going to be with the Father to prepare a place for his followers. He said that he would be returning one day to take his followers with him.

3. What did Jesus promise?

   "Where I am, there ye may be also" (John 14:3b).

4. According to his first letter to Corinth, what did Paul hope our faith would be built upon?

   God's wisdom as opposed to man's wisdom

5. How does giving play a part in our heavenly treasure?*

   Referring to the Memory Verse—Jesus said to him [the rich young man], *"If you would be perfect, go, sell what you possess and give to the poor, and you will have treasure in heaven; and come, follow me"* (Matt. 19:21 ESV). By giving up what he holds valuable on earth and turning to Christ for eternal salvation, the rich young ruler would then possess a heavenly treasure. The main point is that he had to relinquish what was holding him captive, and in this case it was his materialism.

   *Individual answers may vary.

QUESTION 27 ANSWERS:
WHAT DOES GOD SAY HE WILL DO FOR THOSE WHO GIVE?

Bible Study
Luke 12:14-48

But he said unto him, "Man, who made me a judge or a divider over you?" [15] And he said unto them, "Take heed, and keep yourselves from all covetousness:

220

for a man's life consisteth not in the abundance of the things which he possesseth." ¹⁶ And he spake a parable unto them, saying, "The ground of a certain rich man brought forth plentifully: ¹⁷ and he reasoned within himself, saying, What shall I do, because I have not where to bestow my fruits? ¹⁸ And he said, 'This will I do: I will pull down my barns, and build greater; and there will I bestow all my grain and my goods. ¹⁹ And I will say to my soul, Soul, thou hast much goods laid up for many years; take thine ease, eat, drink, be merry.' ²⁰ But God said unto him, 'Thou foolish one, this night is thy soul required of thee; and the things which thou hast prepared, whose shall they be? ²¹ So is he that layeth up treasure for himself, and is not rich toward God.'"

²² And he said unto his disciples, "Therefore I say unto you, Be not anxious for your life, what ye shall eat; nor yet for your body, what ye shall put on. ²³ For the life is more than the food, and the body than the raiment. ²⁴ Consider the ravens, that they sow not, neither reap; which have no store-chamber nor barn; and God feedeth them: of how much more value are ye than the birds! ²⁵ And which of you by being anxious can add a cubit unto the measure of his life? ²⁶ If then ye are not able to do even that which is least, why are ye anxious concerning the rest?" ²⁷ "Consider the lilies, how they grow: they toil not, neither do they spin; yet I say unto you, Even Solomon in all his glory was not arrayed like one of these. ²⁸ But if God doth so clothe the grass in the field, which today is, and tomorrow is cast into the oven; how much more shall he clothe you, O ye of little faith? ²⁹ And seek not ye what ye shall eat, and what ye shall drink, neither be ye of doubtful mind. ³⁰ For all these things do the nations of the world seek after: but your Father knoweth that ye have need of these things. ³¹ Yet seek ye his kingdom, and these things shall be added unto you." ³² "Fear not, little flock; for it is your Father's good pleasure to give you the kingdom. ³³ Sell that which ye have, and give alms; make for yourselves purses which wax not old, a treasure in the heavens that faileth not, where no thief draweth near, neither moth destroyeth. ³⁴ For where your treasure is, there will your heart be also."

³⁵ "Let your loins be girded about, and your lamps burning; ³⁶ and be ye yourselves like unto men looking for their lord, when he shall return from the marriage feast; that, when he cometh and knocketh, they may straightway open unto him. ³⁷ Blessed are those servants, whom the lord when he cometh

shall find watching: verily I say unto you, that he shall gird himself, and make them sit down to meat, and shall come and serve them. [38] And if he shall come in the second watch, and if in the third, and find them so, blessed are those servants. [39] But know this, that if the master of the house had known in what hour the thief was coming, he would have watched, and not have left his house to be broken through. [40] Be ye also ready: for in an hour that ye think not the Son of man cometh."

[41] And Peter said, "Lord, speakest thou this parable unto us, or even unto all?" [42] And the Lord said, "Who then is the faithful and wise steward, whom his lord shall set over his household, to give them their portion of food in due season? [43] Blessed is that servant, whom his lord when he cometh shall find so doing. [44] Of a truth I say unto you, that he will set him over all that he hath. [45] But if that servant shall say in his heart, 'My lord delayeth his coming; and shall begin to beat the menservants and the maidservants, and to eat and drink, and to be drunken'; [46] the lord of that servant shall come in a day when he expecteth not, and in an hour when he knoweth not, and shall cut him asunder, and appoint his portion with the unfaithful." [47] "And that servant, who knew his lord's will, and made not ready, nor did according to his will, shall be beaten with many stripes; [48] but he that knew not, and did things worthy of stripes, shall be beaten with few stripes. And to whomsoever much is given, of him shall much be required: and to whom they commit much, of him will they ask the more."

Bible Study Questions and Answers

1. What was Peter's question to Jesus?
   Peter asked if the parable was only for the disciples or for everyone.

2. How did Jesus answer Peter?
   Jesus answered Peter with another question about who is the faithful steward.

3. In the parable of the faithful steward, what did Jesus say happens to the servant who is found to be faithful and a wise manager, as one doing the will of the master?

   The servant will be blessed and be put over all the master's possessions.

4. Did Jesus answer Peter's questions?

   Yes, Jesus indirectly told Peter that he was speaking to all of those that follow him.

5. In your own words, what is the meaning of Jesus' parable of the faithful steward?*

   We are all stewards of God's possessions and, accordingly, by the world's standards, our lifestyle might be appropriately characterized as having "been given much." This implies that much will be demanded of us from God. And since much has been given to us, God may ask more from us. When we comply through faith, the Lord can entrust more to us.

   *Individual responses may vary.

QUESTION 28 ANSWERS: DOES GOD CHALLENGE US TO GIVE?

Bible Study
Exodus 35; 36:1–7

Exodus 35

And Moses assembled all the congregation of the children of Israel, and said unto them, 'These are the words which Jehovah hath commanded, that ye should do them. ² Six days shall work be done; but on the seventh day there shall be to you a holy day, a sabbath of solemn rest to Jehovah: whosoever doeth any work therein shall be put to death. ³ Ye shall kindle no fire throughout your habitations upon the sabbath day."

[4] And Moses spake unto all the congregation of the children of Israel, saying, "This is the thing which Jehovah commanded, saying, [5] Take ye from among you an offering unto Jehovah; whosoever is of a willing heart, let him bring it, Jehovah's offering: gold, and silver, and brass, [6] and blue, and purple, and scarlet, and fine linen, and goats' hair, [7] and rams' skins dyed red, and sealskins, and acacia wood, [8] and oil for the light, and spices for the anointing oil, and for the sweet incense, [9] and onyx stones, and stones to be set, for the ephod, and for the breastplate."

[10] "And let every wise-hearted man among you come, and make all that Jehovah hath commanded: [11] the tabernacle, its tent, and its covering, its clasps, and its boards, its bars, its pillars, and its sockets; [12] the ark, and the staves thereof, the mercy-seat, and the veil of the screen; [13] the table, and its staves, and all its vessels, and the showbread; [14] the candlestick also for the light, and its vessels, and its lamps, and the oil for the light; [15] and the altar of incense, and its staves, and the anointing oil, and the sweet incense, and the screen for the door, at the door of the tabernacle; [16] the altar of burnt offering, with its grating of brass, its staves, and all its vessels, the laver and its base; [17] the hangings of the court, the pillars thereof, and their sockets, and the screen for the gate of the court; [18] the pins of the tabernacle, and the pins of the court, and their cords; [19] the finely wrought garments, for ministering in the holy place, the holy garments for Aaron the priest, and the garments of his sons, to minister in the priest's office."

[20] And all the congregation of the children of Israel departed from the presence of Moses. [21] And they came, everyone whose heart stirred him up, and every one whom his spirit made willing, and brought Jehovah's offering, for the work of the tent of meeting, and for all the service thereof, and for the holy garments. [22] And they came, both men and women, as many as were willing-hearted, and brought brooches, and earrings, and signet rings, and armlets, all jewels of gold; even every man that offered an offering of gold unto Jehovah. [23] And every man, with whom was found blue, and purple, and scarlet, and fine linen, and goats' hair, and rams' skins dyed red, and sealskins, brought them. [24] Every one that did offer an offering of silver and brass brought Jehovah's offering; and every man, with whom was found acacia wood for any work of the service, brought it. [25] And all the women that

were wise-hearted did spin with their hands, and brought that which they had spun, the blue, and the purple, the scarlet, and the fine linen. ²⁶ And all the women whose heart stirred them up in wisdom spun the goats' hair. ²⁷ And the rulers brought the onyx stones, and the stones to be set, for the ephod, and for the breastplate; ²⁸ and the spice, and the oil; for the light, and for the anointing oil, and for the sweet incense. ²⁹ The children of Israel brought a freewill-offering unto Jehovah; every man and woman, whose heart made them willing to bring for all the work, which Jehovah had commanded to be made by Moses.

³⁰ "And Moses said unto the children of Israel, See, Jehovah hath called by name Bezalel the son of Uri, the son of Hur, of the tribe of Judah; ³¹ and he hath filled him with the Spirit of God, in wisdom, in understanding, and in knowledge, and in all manner of workmanship; ³² and to devise skilful works, to work in gold, and in silver, and in brass, ³³ and in cutting of stones for setting, and in carving of wood, to work in all manner of skilful workmanship. ³⁴ And he hath put in his heart that he may teach, both he, and Oholiab, the son of Ahisamach, of the tribe of Dan. ³⁵ Them hath he filled with wisdom of heart, to work all manner of workmanship, of the engraver, and of the skilful workman, and of the embroiderer, in blue, and in purple, in scarlet, and in fine linen, and of the weaver, even of them that do any workmanship, and of those that devise skilful works."

Exodus 36:1-7

"And Bezalel and Oholiab shall work, and every wise-hearted man, in whom Jehovah hath put wisdom and understanding to know how to work all the work for the service of the sanctuary, according to all that Jehovah hath commanded."

² And Moses called Bezalel and Oholiab, and every wise-hearted man, in whose heart Jehovah had put wisdom, even every one whose heart stirred him up to come unto the work to do it: ³ and they received of Moses all the offering which the children of Israel had brought for the work of the service of the sanctuary, wherewith to make it. And they brought yet unto him freewill-offerings every morning. ⁴ And all the wise men, that wrought all the work of the sanctuary, came every man from his work which they wrought; ⁵ and they spake unto Moses, saying, The people bring much more than enough for the

service of the work which Jehovah commanded to make. ⁶ And Moses gave commandment, and they caused it to be proclaimed throughout the camp, saying, "Let neither man nor woman make any more work for the offering of the sanctuary. So the people were restrained from bringing. ⁷ For the stuff they had was sufficient for all the work to make it, and too much."

Bible Study Questions and Answers

1. Describe what is happening in the setting of Exodus 35?
   Moses is preparing the Israelites for the building of the Tabernacle for the Lord.

2. What is one of the conditions Moses set for those who were to bring forth a contribution of gold, silver, bronze, and other supplies for the Tabernacle?
   They were to have a willing heart.

3. After hearing the supplies needed for building the Tabernacle, what influenced those who returned with supplies?
   They were moved, stirred, or had a willing heart to give.

4. What type of offering did the children of Israel bring for the Lord?
   Free will offering to the Lord (Lord's Contribution is also an appropriate answer.)

5. Who were the two individuals tasked with overseeing the building project?
   Bezalel and Oholiab were employed, as well as other skilled craftsmen.

6. Once the craftsmen were given their respective tasks, what concern did they express to Moses?
   The Israelites brought the craftsmen freewill offerings every morning but not long thereafter the workers had more than enough to complete their work.

7. What common theme is found in the following verses: Exodus 35:5, 21, 22, 26, and 29?

The common theme amongst these verses is the call to those who are willing.

8. What is the significance of the identified common theme?

Generosity starts in our hearts, which is stirred by the Spirit. We are made in God's image and have characteristics that align with the character of God. One such characteristic is giving. The Holy Spirit can move us and the outcome is often-times an overflowing of generosity.

APPLICATION OF GIVING

QUESTION 29 ANSWERS:
WHAT IS SACRIFICIAL GIVING?

Bible Study
Leviticus 6:1-5 and Luke 19:1-10

Leviticus 6:1-5

The Lord said to Moses: [2] "If anyone sins and is unfaithful to the Lord by deceiving a neighbor about something entrusted to them or left in their care or about something stolen, or if they cheat their neighbor, [3] or if they find lost property and lie about it, or if they swear falsely about any such sin that people may commit—[4] when they sin in any of these ways and realize their guilt, they must return what they have stolen or taken by extortion, or what was entrusted to them, or the lost property they found, [5] or whatever it was they swore falsely about. They must make restitution in full, add a fifth of the value to it and give it all to the owner on the day they present their guilt offering."

Luke 19:1-10

And he entered and was passing through Jericho. [2] And behold, a man called by name Zacchaeus; and he was a chief publican, and he was rich. [3] And he sought to see Jesus who he was; and could not for the crowd, because he was little of stature. [4] And he ran on before, and climbed up into a sycamore tree to see him: for he was to pass that way. [5] And when Jesus came to the place, he looked up, and said unto him, "Zacchaeus, make haste, and come down; for today I must abide at thy house." [6] And he made haste, and came down, and received him joyfully. [7] And when they saw it, they all murmured, saying, "He is gone in to lodge with a man that is a sinner." [8] And Zacchaeus stood, and said unto the Lord, "Behold, Lord, the half of my goods I give to the poor; and if I have wrongfully exacted aught of any man, I restore fourfold." [9] And Jesus said unto him, "Today is salvation come to this house, forasmuch as he also is a son of Abraham. [10] For the Son of man came to seek and to save that which was lost."

Bible Study Questions and Answers

1. **Where does the story about Zacchaeus take place?**

   In Jericho. Jesus was travelling to Jerusalem on his final journey before his crucifixion.

2. **What do we know about Zacchaeus?**
   a. He was rich.
   b. He was short.
   c. He was the chief tax collector.

3. **What did the crowd think about Jesus going to the home of Zacchaeus?**

   They were upset because Zacchaeus was considered a sinner and tax collectors were not liked at all, especially the chief tax collector.

4. **After Zacchaeus met with Jesus, what did he proclaim he would do?**

   Zacchaeus declared he would give up half of his wealth (possessions)—giving it to the poor—and he would restore anyone he defrauded four times what he had taken.

5. **Refer to Leviticus 6:1–5. What would Zacchaeus be required to pay according to Levite law?**

   Zacchaeus was only required to repay the full amount plus $1/5^{th}$ or 20% premium over the full amount.

6. **Would Zacchaeus' giving be considered sacrificial?***

   Reflect on giving up to half of everything you own right now and then going around your school or office to pay four times what is owed to others because of past defrauding actions. Zacchaeus' restitution to others could have put him in the poor house! Recall that not only was he a tax collector, he was the chief tax collector. It is likely that when identifying all those he may have wronged, the list was very long. In this story, we see significant sacrifice, or giving up what was needed to rely on Christ!

   *Individual responses may vary.

QUESTION 30 ANSWERS:
PRIOR TO THE OT LAW, WHAT WERE THE ISRAELITES REQUIRED TO GIVE BACK TO THE LORD?

Bible Study
Numbers 18

And Jehovah said unto Aaron, "Thou and thy sons and thy father's' house with thee shall bear the iniquity of the sanctuary; and thou and thy sons with thee shall bear the iniquity of your priesthood. ² And thy brethren also, the tribe of Levi, the tribe of thy father, bring thou near with thee, that they may be joined unto thee, and minister unto thee: but thou and thy sons with thee shall be before the tent of the testimony. ³ And they shall keep thy charge, and the charge of all the Tent: only they shall not come nigh unto the vessels of the sanctuary and unto the altar, that they die not, neither they, nor ye. ⁴ And they shall be joined unto thee, and keep the charge of the tent of meeting, for all the service of the Tent: and a stranger shall not come nigh unto you."

⁵ "And ye shall keep the charge of the sanctuary, and the charge of the altar; that there be wrath no more upon the children of Israel. ⁶ And I, behold, I have taken your brethren the Levites from among the children of Israel: to you they are a gift, given unto Jehovah, to do the service of the tent of meeting. ⁷ And thou and thy sons with thee shall keep your priesthood for everything of the altar, and for that within the veil; and ye shall serve: I give you the priesthood as a service of gift: and the stranger that cometh nigh shall be put to death."

⁸ And Jehovah spake unto Aaron, "And I, behold, I have given thee the charge of my heave-offerings, even all the hallowed things of the children of Israel; unto thee have I given them by reason of the anointing, and to thy sons, as a portion for ever. ⁹ This shall be thine of the most holy things, reserved from the fire: every oblation of theirs, even every meal-offering of theirs, and every sin-offering of theirs, and every trespass-offering of theirs, which they shall render unto me, shall be most holy for thee and for thy sons. ¹⁰ As the most holy things shalt thou eat thereof; every male shall eat thereof: it shall be holy unto thee."

¹¹ "And this is thine: the heave-offering of their gift, even all the wave-offerings of the children of Israel; I have given them unto thee, and to thy sons and to thy daughters with thee, as a portion for ever; every one that is clean in thy house shall eat thereof."

¹² "All the best of the oil, and all the best of the vintage, and of the grain, the firstfruits of them which they give unto Jehovah, to thee have I given them. ¹³ The first-ripe fruits of all that is in their land, which they bring unto Jehovah, shall be thine; every one that is clean in thy house shall eat thereof."

¹⁴ "Everything devoted in Israel shall be thine. ¹⁵ Everything that openeth the womb, of all flesh which they offer unto Jehovah, both of man and beast shall be thine: nevertheless the firstborn of man shalt thou surely redeem, and the firstling of unclean beasts shalt thou redeem. ¹⁶ And those that are to be redeemed of them from a month old shalt thou redeem, according to thine estimation, for the money of five shekels, after the shekel of the sanctuary (the same is twenty gerahs)."

¹⁷ "But the firstling of a cow, or the firstling of a sheep, or the firstling of a goat, thou shalt not redeem; they are holy: thou shalt sprinkle their blood upon the altar, and shalt burn their fat for an offering made by fire, for a sweet savor unto Jehovah. ¹⁸ And the flesh of them shall be thine, as the wave-breast and as the right thigh, it shall be thine. ¹⁹ All the heave-offerings of the holy things, which the children of Israel offer unto Jehovah, have I given thee, and thy sons and thy daughters with thee, as a portion for ever: it is a covenant of salt for ever before Jehovah unto thee and to thy seed with thee."

²⁰ And Jehovah said unto Aaron, "Thou shalt have no inheritance in their land, neither shalt thou have any portion among them: I am thy portion and thine inheritance among the children of Israel."

²¹ "And unto the children of Levi, behold, I have given all the tithe in Israel for an inheritance, in return for their service which they serve, even the service of the tent of meeting. ²² And henceforth the children of Israel shall not come nigh the tent of meeting, lest they bear sin, and die. ²³ But the Levites shall do the service of the tent of meeting, and they shall bear their iniquity: it shall

be a statute for ever throughout your generations; and among the children of Israel they shall have no inheritance. ²⁴ For the tithe of the children of Israel, which they offer as a heave-offering unto Jehovah, I have given to the Levites for an inheritance: therefore I have said unto them, 'Among the children of Israel they shall have no inheritance.'"

²⁵ And Jehovah spake unto Moses, saying, ²⁶ "Moreover thou shalt speak unto the Levites, and say unto them, 'When ye take of the children of Israel the tithe which I have given you from them for your inheritance, then ye shall offer up a heave-offering of it for Jehovah, a tithe of the tithe. ²⁷ And your heave-offering shall be reckoned unto you, as though it were the grain of the threshing-floor, and as the fulness of the winepress. ²⁸ Thus ye also shall offer a heave-offering unto Jehovah of all your tithes, which ye receive of the children of Israel; and thereof ye shall give Jehovah's heave-offering to Aaron the priest. ²⁹ Out of all your gifts ye shall offer every heave-offering of Jehovah, of all the best thereof, even the hallowed part thereof out of it.'"

³⁰ "Therefore thou shalt say unto them, 'When ye heave the best thereof from it, then it shall be reckoned unto the Levites as the increase of the threshing-floor, and as the increase of the winepress. ³¹ And ye shall eat it in every place, ye and your households: for it is your reward in return for your service in the tent of meeting. ³² And ye shall bear no sin by reason of it, when ye have heaved from it the best thereof: and ye shall not profane the holy things of the children of Israel, that ye die not.'"

Bible Study Questions and Answers

1. What did the Lord tell Aaron that he and his son's would bear from the Lord's people?

   Iniquity connected to the sanctuary and iniquity connected to the priesthood

2. What was the responsibility of the tribe of Levi?

   The Levite tribe was responsible for keeping guard over the people of Israel and over the whole tent of meeting, the sanctuary, and the altar.

3. What did the Lord give Aaron and the tribe Levi charge over?

The Levites received the contributions made to the Lord by the people of Israel and all the consecrated things.

4. Which offerings were the Levi tribe given?

All the offerings made were given to the Levite tribe, every: (a) grain offering, (b) sin offering, (c) guilt offering, and (d) wave offering.

5. Was there anything else given to the Levi tribe?
   a. The firstfruits of what the Israelites gave to the Lord
   b. Every devoted thing in Israel
   c. Everything that opened the womb of all flesh (man or beast)

6. What was the inheritance supposed to be for the tribe of Levi?

The tribe of Levi was not to receive an inheritance; the Lord was their portion and inheritance.

7. In addition to the offerings, what else did the Lord give to the Levites?

The Lord gave the Levites every tithe in Israel for their service in the tent of meeting.

8. Where there any conditions the Levites needed to follow related to the tithe?

The Levites were to tithe on the amounts received by the people of Israel, called a tithe of the tithe.

QUESTION 32 ANSWERS:
WHAT IS TO BE OUR FIRST FINANCIAL PRIORITY?

Bible Study
I Corinthians 16:1-4

Now concerning the collection for the saints, as I gave order to the churches of Galatia, so also do ye. [2] Upon the first day of the week let each one of you lay by him in store, as he may prosper, that no collections be made when I come. [3] And when I arrive, whomsoever ye shall approve, them will I send with letters to carry your bounty unto Jerusalem: [4] and if it be meet for me to go also, they shall go with me.

Bible Study Questions

1. Why do you think Paul starts 1 Corinthians 16 with "Now concerning?"*

    Similar to 1 Corinthians 7:1 and 12:1, we see Paul addressing questions that this young church at Corinth had.

2. What was Paul addressing in the early part of his letter to the Corinthians?

    Paul was gathering a collection for the poor in Jerusalem. There was a severe famine in Jerusalem.

3. How often did Paul suggest the church in Corinth take collection?

    On the first day of each week, they were to put money aside that had been stored up.

4. Why do you think Paul declared the first day of each week as the time to set aside their tithe?*

    This may have been suggested to create a systematic process to continually remind those in the church of their stewardship role.

5. How much were the Corinthians supposed to set aside?

    Paul is vague in his answer. He states that the people were to set aside in keeping with their prosperity. What this means for us is that we are to set aside money based upon how much God has provided to us.

*Individual responses may vary.

QUESTION 33 ANSWERS:
IS THERE A PATTERN OF GIVING WE SHOULD FOLLOW?

Bible Study
Luke 22:14-23

And when the hour was come, he sat down, and the apostles with him. [15] And he said unto them, "With desire I have desired to eat this passover with you before I suffer: [16] for I say unto you, I shall not eat it, until it be fulfilled in the kingdom of God." [17] And he received a cup, and when he had given thanks, he said, "Take this, and divide it among yourselves: [18] for I say unto you, I shall not drink from henceforth of the fruit of the vine, until the kingdom of God shall come." [19] And he took bread, and when he had given thanks, he brake it, and gave to them, saying, "This is my body which is given for you: this do in remembrance of me." [20] And the cup in like manner after supper, saying, "This cup is the new covenant in my blood, even that which is poured out for you. [21] But behold, the hand of him that betrayeth me is with me on the table. [22] For the Son of man indeed goeth, as it hath been determined: but woe unto that man through whom he is betrayed!" [23] And they began to question among themselves, which of them it was that should do this thing.

Bible Study Questions and Answers

1. What is taking place in the Luke 22 passage?
   Jesus and his disciples are taking part in the Passover supper right before Jesus is about to be handed over to the Romans; it is the Lord's Supper.

2. What did Jesus partake of first and then pass around to his disciples?
   A cup with drink from the fruit of the vine

3. What did Jesus partake of second and then pass around to his disciples?
   Bread

4. What did Jesus say to his disciples after breaking the bread?
   "This is my body, which is given for you. This do in remembrance of me" (Luke 22:19).

5. Why did Jesus command his disciples to take part in the remembrance of the Lord's Supper?*

   We are naturally forgetful people and constantly need to be reminded of even the most important things. Jesus tells his disciples to do this ritual of breaking bread to remember the very sacrifice that he was making on behalf of all. We require continual reminding of our need for salvation and that our salvation comes from the broken body of Christ when he died on the cross.

   Individual responses may vary.

QUESTION 34 ANSWERS: WHO SHOULD WE GIVE TO?

Bible Study

Acts 4

And as they spake unto the people, the priests and the captain of the temple and the Sadducees came upon them, ² being sore troubled because they taught the people, and proclaimed in Jesus the resurrection from the dead. ³ And they laid hands on them, and put them in ward unto the morrow: for it was now eventide. ⁴ But many of them that heard the word believed; and the number of the men came to be about five thousand.

⁵ And it came to pass on the morrow, that their rulers and elders and scribes were gathered together in Jerusalem; ⁶ and Annas the high priest was there, and Caiaphas, and John, and Alexander, and as many as were of the kindred of the high priest. ⁷ And when they had set them in the midst, they inquired, "By what power, or in what name, have ye done this?" ⁸ Then Peter, filled with the Holy Spirit, said unto them, "Ye rulers of the people, and elders, ⁹ if we this day are examined concerning a good deed done to an impotent man, by what means this man is made whole; ¹⁰ be it known unto you all, and to all

the people of Israel, that in the name of Jesus Christ of Nazareth, whom ye crucified, whom God raised from the dead, even by him doth this man stand here before you whole. [11] He is the stone which was set at nought of you the builders, which was made the head of the corner. [12] And in none other is there salvation: for neither is there any other name under heaven, that is given among men, wherein we must be saved."

[13] Now when they beheld the boldness of Peter and John, and had perceived that they were unlearned and ignorant men, they marvelled; and they took knowledge of them, that they had been with Jesus. [14] And seeing the man that was healed standing with them, they could say nothing against it. [15] But when they had commanded them to go aside out of the council, they conferred among themselves, [16] saying, "What shall we do to these men? for that indeed a notable miracle hath been wrought through them, is manifest to all that dwell in Jerusalem; and we cannot deny it. [17] But that it spread no further among the people, let us threaten them, that they speak henceforth to no man in this name." [18] And they called them, and charged them not to speak at all nor teach in the name of Jesus. [19] But Peter and John answered and said unto them, "Whether it is right in the sight of God to hearken unto you rather than unto God, judge ye: [20] for we cannot but speak the things which we saw and heard." [21] And they, when they had further threatened them, let them go, finding nothing how they might punish them, because of the people; for all men glorified God for that which was done. [22] For the man was more than forty years old, on whom this miracle of healing was wrought.

[23] And being let go, they came to their own company, and reported all that the chief priests and the elders had said unto them. [24] And they, when they heard it, lifted up their voice to God with one accord, and said, "O Lord, thou that didst make the heaven and the earth and the sea, and all that in them is: [25] who by the Holy Spirit, by the mouth of our father David thy servant, didst say,

'Why did the Gentiles rage,
And the peoples imagine vain things?
[26] The kings of the earth set themselves in array,
And the rulers were gathered together,
Against the Lord, and against his Anointed:'

²⁷ for of a truth in this city against thy holy Servant Jesus, whom thou didst anoint, both Herod and Pontius Pilate, with the Gentiles and the peoples of Israel, were gathered together, ²⁸ to do whatsoever thy hand and thy council foreordained to come to pass. ²⁹ And now, Lord, look upon their threatenings: and grant unto thy servants to speak thy word with all boldness, ³⁰ while thou stretchest forth thy hand to heal; and that signs and wonders may be done through the name of thy holy Servant Jesus." ³¹ And when they had prayed, the place was shaken wherein they were gathered together; and they were all filled with the Holy Spirit, and they spake the word of God with boldness.

³² And the multitude of them that believed were of one heart and soul: and not one of them said that aught of the things which he possessed was his own; but they had all things common. ³³ And with great power gave the apostles their witness of the resurrection of the Lord Jesus: and great grace was upon them all. ³⁴ For neither was there among them any that lacked: for as many as were possessors of lands or houses sold them, and brought the prices of the things that were sold, ³⁵ and laid them at the apostles' feet: and distribution was made unto each, according as any one had need.

³⁶ And Joseph, who by the apostles was surnamed Barnabas (which is, being interpreted, Son of exhortation), a Levite, a man of Cyprus by race, ³⁷ having a field, sold it, and brought the money and laid it at the apostles' feet.

Bible Study Questions and Answers

1. In general, what is taking place at the beginning of Acts 4?
   Peter and John are proclaiming the resurrection of Jesus.

2. What did the Priests and Sadducees do as a result of the actions of Peter and John?
   They put Peter and John in jail overnight.

3. According to the reading, how many heard and believed the proclamations of Peter and John?
   About 5,000 men

4. When Peter and John were on trial the next day, what did the people see in them?
   Boldness

5. Peter and John were released on what condition? Did they agree?
   a. They were not to speak or teach at all in the name of Jesus.
   b. No, Peter and John did not agree with the conditions for their release; instead, they said, "we cannot but speak of what we have seen and heard."

6. Peter and John went back to their fellow believers and prayed for continued boldness. What happened next?
   After they prayed, the place shook and they were all filled with the Holy Spirit and continued to speak the Word of God with boldness.

7. What was the first revelation that occurred after the Holy Spirit filled everyone?
   The people realized they did not own anything that belonged to them, and that they had everything in common.

8. What did the people do as a result of the first revelation? And, what did it accomplish?
   If they owned land or houses, they sold them and brought the proceeds from what was sold and laid it at the apostles' feet. There was not a needy person among them because the proceeds were distributed to each as any had a need.

QUESTION 35 ANSWERS:
DO WE NEED TO BE CAUTIOUS IN OUR GIVING?

Bible Study
Romans 16:17–20

Now I beseech you, brethren, mark them that are causing the divisions and occasions of stumbling, contrary to the doctrine which ye learned: and turn away from them. [18] For they that are such serve not our Lord Christ, but their own belly; and by their smooth and fair speech they beguile the hearts of the innocent. [19] For your obedience is come abroad unto all men. I rejoice therefore over you: but I would have you wise unto that which is good, and simple unto that which is evil. [20] And the God of peace shall bruise Satan under your feet shortly.

The grace of our Lord Jesus Christ be with you.

Bible Study Questions and Answers

1. This section of Scripture is wrapping up one of Paul's most famous letters. What does Paul appeal to the brothers to do?
   a. Watch out for those who cause divisions and create obstacles contrary to the doctrine that you have been taught.
   b. Paul also says to avoid them.

2. What does Paul say that individuals causing divisions and occasions for stumbling are doing and not doing?
   a. They do not serve the Lord.
   b. They serve their own appetite.

3. Of those who are causing divisions, how are they doing it?
   a. They use smooth talk.
   b. They use flattery.
   c. They deceive the hearts of the naïve.

4. Although Paul is optimistic regarding the obedience of his audience, what is his desire for them?
   To be wise as to what is good and innocent and as to what is evil

5. Based on Romans 16:20, who is ultimately responsible for the divisions and occasions for stumbling?
   Paul points to Satan, but the God of Peace will soon crush Satan.

QUESTION 36 ANSWERS:
WHAT ARE THE BENEFITS OF GIVING TO OTHERS?

Bible Study

1 Peter 2:24-25; 4:13 and Colossians 1:21-22

Colossians 1:21-22

And you, being in time past alienated and enemies in your mind in your evil works, [22] yet now hath he reconciled in the body of his flesh through death, to present you holy and without blemish and unreproveable before him:

1 Peter 2:24-25

who his own self bare our sins in his body upon the tree, that we, having died unto sins, might live unto righteousness; by whose stripes ye were healed. [25] For ye were going astray like sheep; but are now returned unto the Shepherd and Bishop of your souls.

1 Peter 4:13

But rejoice inasmuch as you participate in the sufferings of Christ, so that you may be overjoyed when his glory is revealed.

Bible Study Questions and Answers

1. In 1 Peter 2:24, who is Peter talking about suffering?
   Christ

2. According to Peter, what did Christ give up for us?
   Jesus gave up his body on the cross.

3. What does Peter say was the purpose of Christ's death?
   So that we might die to sins and live for righteousness

4. According to Paul, what was our state of being before Christ gave us salvation?
   Before Christ saved us, we were against God; we were his enemies because of our sin.

5. How were we reconciled back to God?
   Through the death of Christ's physical body and his victory over death, he presents us as holy in God's sight.

6. What did Jesus ultimately give us that satisfies all our needs?*
   Jesus took our place on the cross—dying for our sins—so that we, through a repentant heart and believing faith, might receive his righteousness upon our lives. Accordingly, Christ provides for our needs, answers our prayers, gives us honor, and blesses our work.

*Individual responses may vary.

BUDGETING

QUESTION 37 ANSWERS:
WHAT IS THE BIBLICAL PURPOSE OF A BUDGET?

Bible Study
Luke 14:26–32

"If any man cometh unto me, and hateth not his own father, and mother, and wife, and children, and brethren, and sisters, yea, and his own life also, he cannot be my disciple. [27] Whosoever doth not bear his own cross, and come after me, cannot be my disciple."

[28] "For which of you, desiring to build a tower, doth not first sit down and count the cost, whether he have wherewith to complete it? [29] Lest haply, when he hath laid a foundation, and is not able to finish, all that behold begin to mock him, [30] saying, 'This man began to build, and was not able to finish.'"

[31] "Or what king, as he goeth to encounter another king in war, will not sit down first and take counsel whether he is able with ten thousand to meet him that cometh against him with twenty thousand? [32] Or else, while the other is yet a great way off, he sendeth an ambassage, and asketh conditions of peace."

Bible Study Questions and Answers

1. What is the heading in your Bible for the Luke 14:26–32 passage, if one is available?
   "The Cost of Discipleship" is shown in the NIV. Headings will vary by Bible version.

2. Why do you think Jesus starts talking to the crowds about hating their own family members?*
   Jesus was emphasizing the importance that we must put on him in order to be a disciple, one who fully follows his teachings.

3. Besides "hating" one's family, what else must we do to be a follower of Christ?

We must carry our own cross and come after Christ in order to be his disciple.

4. When sharing the parable about the concept of knowing the cost, what example does Jesus use?

Jesus shares the example of building a tower, and the need to sit down to plan and count the cost.

5. What is Jesus implying when he refers to "counting the cost"?

This is in essence "budgeting." Christ emphasizes the importance of establishing goals and identifying the tasks to be completed and that, in order to achieve our goals, we need to prepare in advance for the costs to accomplish them.

6. What is the outcome if we are unable to complete our task due to a lack of planning?

We could be mocked or ridiculed.

7. What other example of counting cost did Jesus share?

Jesus also likens this to a king who does not plan his attack on his enemies in war to determine how many soldiers he needs.

8. How does Jesus finish this set of parables?

Jesus tells us that if we do not renounce all that we have we cannot be his disciple.

*Individual responses may vary.

QUESTION 38 ANSWERS:
WHAT DOES BUDGETING OUR FINANCES DO FOR US?

Bible Study
Job 38–41

Then Jehovah answered Job out of the whirlwind, and said,
²"Who is this that darkeneth counsel
By words without knowledge?
³Gird up now thy loins like a man;

243

For I will demand of thee, and declare thou unto me."
⁴"Where wast thou when I laid the foundations of the earth?
Declare, if thou hast understanding.
⁵Who determined the measures thereof, if thou knowest?
Or who stretched the line upon it?
⁶Whereupon were the foundations thereof fastened?
Or who laid the corner-stone thereof,
⁷When the morning stars sang together,
And all the sons of God shouted for joy?"
⁸"Or who shut up the sea with doors,
When it brake forth, as if it had issued out of the womb;
⁹When I made clouds the garment thereof,
And thick darkness a swaddling-band for it,
¹⁰And marked out for it my bound,
And set bars and doors,
¹¹And said, Hitherto shalt thou come, but no further;
And here shall thy proud waves be stayed?"
¹²"Hast thou commanded the morning since thy days began,
And caused the dayspring to know its place;
¹³That it might take hold of the ends of the earth,
And the wicked be shaken out of it?
¹⁴It is changed as clay under the seal;
And all things stand forth as a garment:
¹⁵And from the wicked their light is withholden,
And the high arm is broken."
¹⁶"Hast thou entered into the springs of the sea?
Or hast thou walked in the recesses of the deep?
¹⁷Have the gates of death been revealed unto thee?
Or hast thou seen the gates of the shadow of death?
¹⁸Hast thou comprehended the earth in its breadth?
Declare, if thou knowest it all."
¹⁹"Where is the way to the dwelling of light?
And as for darkness, where is the place thereof,
²⁰That thou shouldest take it to the bound thereof,
And that thou shouldest discern the paths to the house thereof?

²¹*Doubtless, thou knowest, for thou wast then born,*
And the number of thy days is great!
²²*Hast thou entered the treasuries of the snow,*
Or hast thou seen the treasures of the hail,
²³*Which I have reserved against the time of trouble,*
Against the day of battle and war?
²⁴*By what way is the light parted,*
Or the east wind scattered upon the earth?"
²⁵*"Who hath cleft a channel for the waterflood,*
Or the way for the lightning of the thunder;
²⁶*To cause it to rain on a land where no man is;*
On the wilderness, wherein there is no man;
²⁷*To satisfy the waste and desolate ground,*
And to cause the tender grass to spring forth?
²⁸*Hath the rain a father?*
Or who hath begotten the drops of dew?
²⁹*Out of whose womb came the ice?*
And the hoary frost of heaven, who hath gendered it?
³⁰*The waters hide themselves and become like stone,*
And the face of the deep is frozen."
³¹*"Canst thou bind the cluster of the Pleiades,*
Or loose the bands of Orion?
³²*Canst thou lead forth the Mazzaroth in their season?*
Or canst thou guide the Bear with her train?
³³*Knowest thou the ordinances of the heavens?*
Canst thou establish the dominion thereof in the earth?"
³⁴*"Canst thou lift up thy voice to the clouds,*
That abundance of waters may cover thee?
³⁵*Canst thou send forth lightnings, that they may go,*
And say unto thee, Here we are?
³⁶*Who hath put wisdom in the inward parts?*
Or who hath given understanding to the mind?
³⁷*Who can number the clouds by wisdom?*
Or who can pour out the bottles of heaven,
³⁸*When the dust runneth into a mass,*

And the clods cleave fast together?"

³⁹ "Canst thou hunt the prey for the lioness,

Or satisfy the appetite of the young lions,

⁴⁰ When they couch in their dens,

And abide in the covert to lie in wait?

⁴¹ Who provideth for the raven his prey,

When his young ones cry unto God,

And wander for lack of food?"

³⁹ "Knowest thou the time when the wild goats of the rock bring forth?

Or canst thou mark when the hinds do calve?

² Canst thou number the months that they fulfil?

Or knowest thou the time when they bring forth?

³ They bow themselves, they bring forth their young,

They cast out their pains.

⁴ Their young ones become strong, they grow up in the open field;

They go forth, and return not again."

⁵ "Who hath sent out the wild ass free?

Or who hath loosed the bonds of the swift ass,

⁶ Whose home I have made the wilderness,

And the salt land his dwelling-place?

⁷ He scorneth the tumult of the city,

Neither heareth he the shoutings of the driver.

⁸ The range of the mountains is his pasture,

And he searcheth after every green thing.

⁹ Will the wild-ox be content to serve thee?

Or will he abide by thy crib?

¹⁰ Canst thou bind the wild-ox with his band in the furrow?

Or will he harrow the valleys after thee?

¹¹ Wilt thou trust him, because his strength is great?

Or wilt thou leave to him thy labor?

¹² Wilt thou confide in him, that he will bring home thy seed,

And gather the grain of thy threshing-floor?"

¹³ "The wings of the ostrich wave proudly;

But are they the pinions and plumage of love?

¹⁴ For she leaveth her eggs on the earth,

And warmeth them in the dust,

¹⁵And forgetteth that the foot may crush them,

Or that the wild beast may trample them.

¹⁶She dealeth hardly with her young ones, as if they were not hers:

Though her labor be in vain, she is without fear;

¹⁷Because God hath deprived her of wisdom,

Neither hath he imparted to her understanding.

¹⁸What time she lifteth up herself on high,

She scorneth the horse and his rider."

¹⁹"Hast thou given the horse his might?

Hast thou clothed his neck with the quivering mane?

²⁰Hast thou made him to leap as a locust?

The glory of his snorting is terrible.

²¹He paweth in the valley, and rejoiceth in his strength:

He goeth out to meet the armed men.

²²He mocketh at fear, and is not dismayed;

Neither turneth he back from the sword.

²³The quiver rattleth against him,

The flashing spear and the javelin.

²⁴He swalloweth the ground with fierceness and rage;

Neither believeth he that it is the voice of the trumpet.

²⁵As oft as the trumpet soundeth he saith, Aha!

And he smelleth the battle afar off,

The thunder of the captains, and the shouting."

²⁶"Is it by thy wisdom that the hawk soareth,

And stretcheth her wings toward the south?

²⁷Is it at thy command that the eagle mounteth up,

And maketh her nest on high?

²⁸On the cliff she dwelleth, and maketh her home,

Upon the point of the cliff, and the stronghold.

²⁹From thence she spieth out the prey;

Her eyes behold it afar off.

³⁰Her young ones also suck up blood:

And where the slain are, there is she."

⁴⁰ "Moreover Jehovah answered Job, and said,

²*Shall he that cavilleth contend with the Almighty?*
He that argueth with God, let him answer it.
³*"Then Job answered Jehovah, and said,*
⁴*Behold, I am of small account; what shall I answer thee?*
I lay my hand upon my mouth.
⁵*Once have I spoken, and I will not answer;*
Yea, twice, but I will proceed no further."
⁶*"Then Jehovah answered Job out of the whirlwind, and said,*
⁷*Gird up thy loins now like a man:*
I will demand of thee, and declare thou unto me.
⁸*Wilt thou even annul my judgment?*
Wilt thou condemn me, that thou mayest be justified?
⁹*Or hast thou an arm like God?*
And canst thou thunder with a voice like him?"
¹⁰*"Deck thyself now with excellency and dignity;*
And array thyself with honor and majesty.
¹¹*Pour forth the overflowings of thine anger;*
And look upon every one that is proud, and abase him.
¹²*Look on every one that is proud, and bring him low;*
And tread down the wicked where they stand.
¹³*Hide them in the dust together;*
Bind their faces in the hidden place.
¹⁴*Then will I also confess of thee*
That thine own right hand can save thee."
¹⁵*"Behold now, behemoth, which I made as well as thee;*
He eateth grass as an ox.
¹⁶*Lo now, his strength is in his loins,*
And his force is in the muscles of his belly.
¹⁷*He moveth his tail like a cedar:*
The sinews of his thighs are knit together.
¹⁸*His bones are as tubes of brass;*
His limbs are like bars of iron."
¹⁹*"He is the chief of the ways of God:*
He only that made him giveth him his sword.
²⁰*Surely the mountains bring him forth food,*

Where all the beasts of the field do play.
²¹He lieth under the lotus-trees,
In the covert of the reed, and the fen.
²²The lotus-trees cover him with their shade;
The willows of the brook compass him about.
²³Behold, if a river overflow, he trembleth not;
He is confident, though a Jordan swell even to his mouth.
²⁴Shall any take him when he is on the watch,
Or pierce through his nose with a snare?"
⁴¹ "Canst thou draw out leviathan with a fishhook?
Or press down his tongue with a cord?
²Canst thou put a rope into his nose?
Or pierce his jaw through with a hook?
³Will he make many supplications unto thee?
Or will he speak soft words unto thee?
⁴Will he make a covenant with thee,
That thou shouldest take him for a servant for ever?
⁵Wilt thou play with him as with a bird?
Or wilt thou bind him for thy maidens?
⁶Will the bands of fishermen make traffic of him?
Will they part him among the merchants?
⁷Canst thou fill his skin with barbed irons,
Or his head with fish-spears?
⁸Lay thy hand upon him;
Remember the battle, and do so no more.
⁹Behold, the hope of him is in vain:
Will not one be cast down even at the sight of him?
¹⁰None is so fierce that he dare stir him up;
Who then is he that can stand before me?"
¹¹"Who hath first given unto me, that I should repay him?
Whatsoever is under the whole heaven is mine."
¹²"I will not keep silence concerning his limbs,
Nor his mighty strength, nor his goodly frame.
¹³Who can strip off his outer garment?
Who shall come within his jaws?

¹⁴Who can open the doors of his face?
Round about his teeth is terror.
¹⁵His strong scales are his pride,
Shut up together as with a close seal.
¹⁶One is so near to another,
That no air can come between them.
¹⁷They are joined one to another;
They stick together, so that they cannot be sundered.
¹⁸His sneezings flash forth light,
And his eyes are like the eyelids of the morning.
¹⁹Out of his mouth go burning torches,
And sparks of fire leap forth.
²⁰Out of his nostrils a smoke goeth,
As of a boiling pot and burning rushes.
²¹His breath kindleth coals,
And a flame goeth forth from his mouth.
²²In his neck abideth strength,
And terror danceth before him.
²³The flakes of his flesh are joined together:
They are firm upon him; they cannot be moved.
²⁴His heart is as firm as a stone;
Yea, firm as the nether millstone.
²⁵When he raiseth himself up, the mighty are afraid:
By reason of consternation they are beside themselves.
²⁶If one lay at him with the sword, it cannot avail;
Nor the spear, the dart, nor the pointed shaft.
²⁷He counteth iron as straw,
And brass as rotten wood.
²⁸The arrow cannot make him flee:
Sling-stones are turned with him into stubble.
²⁹Clubs are counted as stubble:
He laugheth at the rushing of the javelin.
³⁰His underparts are like sharp potsherds:
He spreadeth as it were a threshing-wain upon the mire.
³¹He maketh the deep to boil like a pot:

He maketh the sea like a pot of ointment.
³²He maketh a path to shine after him;
One would think the deep to be hoary.
³³Upon earth there is not his like,
That is made without fear.
³⁴He beholdeth everything that is high:
He is king over all the sons of pride."

Bible Study Questions and Answers

1. What does God claim Job is doing? Why is what Job is doing inappropriate?

    God suggests that Job is obscuring his plans with words and he is doing it without knowledge.

2. Provide the verses to each activity God does that includes order:
    a. God marked off dimensions of the earth (Job 38:5).
    b. He shut up the sea behind doors when it burst forth from the womb (Job 38:8).
    c. God entered the storehouses of the snow or seen the storehouses of the hail (Job 38:22).
    d. He brings the constellations in their seasons (Job 38:32).
    e. God knows the laws of the heavens (Job 38:33).
    f. He gave the horse its strength or clothed its neck with a flowing mane (Job 39:19).

3. After reading these few chapters of God's response to Job, how do you feel about the way God wants us to handle his resources?*

    Since God is a god of order, he would expect us to manage his money in an orderly fashion. The way we can do this is through a budget which we can answer the questions God may ask us about how we use the financial resources he allows us to use.

*Individual answers may vary.

QUESTION 39 ANSWERS:
HOW ARE WE TO GET STARTED WHEN CREATING A BUDGET?

Discussion Question

1. What were your first thoughts as you finished the interview with your pastor?*

2. Did any part of the conversation make you feel uncomfortable? If so, explain.*

3. Based on what you have learned, how has your view of money changed, if any?*

4. How has what you learned influenced the way you plan on managing money in the future?*

*Individual answers will vary.

SAVING MONEY

QUESTION 40 ANSWERS:
DOES SAVING MONEY GO AGAINST SCRIPTURE?

Bible Study
Matthew 24:42-43; Luke 12:35-38, 21:36; 1 Corinthians 16:13; Colossians 4:2; and 1 Thessalonians 5:6

Matthew 24:42-43

"Watch therefore: for ye know not on what day your Lord cometh. [43]But know this, that if the master of the house had known in what watch the thief was coming, he would have watched, and would not have suffered his house to be broken through."

Luke 12:35-38

"Let your loins be girded about, and your lamps burning; [36]and be ye yourselves like unto men looking for their lord, when he shall return from the marriage feast; that, when he cometh and knocketh, they may straightway open unto him. [37]Blessed are those servants, whom the lord when he cometh shall find watching: verily I say unto you, that he shall gird himself, and make them sit down to meat, and shall come and serve them. [38]And if he shall come in the second watch, and if in the third, and find them so, blessed are those servants."

Luke 21:36

"But watch ye at every season, making supplication, that ye may prevail to escape all these things that shall come to pass, and to stand before the Son of man."

1 Corinthians 16:13

Watch ye, stand fast in the faith, quit you like men, be strong.

Colossians 4:2

Continue steadfastly in prayer, watching therein with thanksgiving;

1 Thessalonians 5:6

So then let us not sleep, as others do, but let us keep awake and be sober.

Bible Study Questions and Answers

1. What do all of the Bible Study passages have in common?
   They all speak to be alert and prepared.

2. What do the Bible Study passages teach us about saving?*
   Setting money aside is one way we can be prepared for what might come. This is not referring to the return of Christ, but rather helping to minimize the worries of tomorrow (Matt. 6:34).

3. In Luke's gospel, how does saving money help us to "be ready?"
   Having money set aside for emergencies or other instances of spiritual conviction can be used when the Holy Spirit prompts us to action. These may be actions of generosity or, perhaps, a job transfer that would only be possible with money set aside to use during such times.

4. In both Colossians and 1 Corinthians, we see God's Word proclaim to be on guard or watchful. How does saving money apply to being watchful or on guard?
   Saving money can allow us to be on guard against life's emergencies. Like a watchman that is looking out for those under their care, money that is saved can help protect us from unknown events in our life.

*Individual responses may vary.

QUESTION 41 ANSWERS:
WHAT DO WE NEED TO BE CAUTIOUS ABOUT WHEN SAVING?

Bible Study
Daniel 4

Nebuchadnezzar the king, unto all the peoples, nations, and languages, that dwell in all the earth: Peace be multiplied unto you. ²It hath seemed good unto me to show the signs and wonders that the Most High God hath wrought toward me.

> ³*How great are his signs!*
> *and how mighty are his wonders!*
> *his kingdom is an everlasting kingdom,*
> *and his dominion is from generation to generation.*

⁴I, Nebuchadnezzar, was at rest in my house, and flourishing in my palace. ⁵I saw a dream which made me afraid; and the thoughts upon my bed and the visions of my head troubled me. ⁶Therefore made I a decree to bring in all the wise men of Babylon before me, that they might make known unto me the interpretation of the dream. ⁷Then came in the magicians, the enchanters, the Chaldeans, and the soothsayers; and I told the dream before them; but they did not make known unto me the interpretation thereof. ⁸But at the last Daniel came in before me, whose name was Belteshazzar, according to the name of my god, and in whom is the spirit of the holy gods: and I told the dream before him, saying, ⁹"O Belteshazzar, master of the magicians, because I know that the spirit of the holy gods is in thee, and no secret troubleth thee, tell me the visions of my dream that I have seen, and the interpretation thereof." ¹⁰Thus were the visions of my head upon my bed: I saw, and, behold, a tree in the midst of the earth; and the height thereof was great. ¹¹The tree grew, and was strong, and the height thereof reached unto heaven, and the sight thereof to the end of all the earth. ¹²The leaves thereof were fair, and the fruit thereof much, and in it was food for all: the beasts of the field had shadow under it, and the birds of the heavens dwelt in the branches thereof, and all flesh was fed from it." ¹³"I saw in the visions of my head upon my bed, and, behold, a

watcher and a holy one came down from heaven. [14]He cried aloud, and said thus, 'Hew down the tree, and cut off its branches, shake off its leaves, and scatter its fruit: let the beasts get away from under it, and the fowls from its branches. [15]Nevertheless leave the stump of its roots in the earth, even with a band of iron and brass, in the tender grass of the field; and let it be wet with the dew of heaven: and let his portion be with the beasts in the grass of the earth: [16]let his heart be changed from man's, and let a beast's heart be given unto him; and let seven times pass over him. [17]"The sentence is by the decree of the watchers, and the demand by the word of the holy ones; to the intent that the living may know that the Most High ruleth in the kingdom of men, and giveth it to whomsoever he will, and setteth up over it the lowest of men.'" [18]"This dream I, king Nebuchadnezzar, have seen; and thou, O Belteshazzar, declare the interpretation, forasmuch as all the wise men of my kingdom are not able to make known unto me the interpretation; but thou art able; for the spirit of the holy gods is in thee."

[19]Then Daniel, whose name was Belteshazzar, was stricken dumb for a while, and his thoughts troubled him. The king answered and said, "Belteshazzar, let not the dream, or the interpretation, trouble thee." Belteshazzar answered and said, "My lord, the dream be to them that hate thee, and the interpretation thereof to thine adversaries. [20]The tree that thou sawest, which grew, and was strong, whose height reached unto heaven, and the sight thereof to all the earth; [21]whose leaves were fair, and the fruit thereof much, and in it was food for all; under which the beasts of the field dwelt, and upon whose branches the birds of the heavens had their habitation: [22]it is thou, O king, that art grown and become strong; for thy greatness is grown, and reacheth unto heaven, and thy dominion to the end of the earth." [23]"And whereas the king saw a watcher and a holy one coming down from heaven, and saying, 'Hew down the tree, and destroy it; nevertheless leave the stump of the roots thereof in the earth, even with a band of iron and brass, in the tender grass of the field, and let it be wet with the dew of heaven: and let his portion be with the beasts of the field, till seven times pass over him'; [24]this is the interpretation, O king, and it is the decree of the Most High, which is come upon my lord the king: [25]that thou shalt be driven from men, and thy dwelling shall be with the beasts of the field, and thou shalt be made to eat grass as oxen, and shalt be wet with the dew of heaven, and seven times shall pass over thee; till thou know that the

Most High ruleth in the kingdom of men, and giveth it to whomsoever he will. [26]And whereas they commanded to leave the stump of the roots of the tree; thy kingdom shall be sure unto thee, after that thou shalt have known that the heavens do rule. [27]Wherefore, O king, let my counsel be acceptable unto thee, and break off thy sins by righteousness, and thine iniquities by showing mercy to the poor; if there may be a lengthening of thy tranquillity."

[28]All this came upon the king Nebuchadnezzar. [29]At the end of twelve months he was walking in the royal palace of Babylon. [30]The king spake and said, Is not this great Babylon, which I have built for the royal dwelling-place, by the might of my power and for the glory of my majesty? [31]While the word was in the king's mouth, there fell a voice from heaven, saying, O king Nebuchadnezzar, to thee it is spoken: The kingdom is departed from thee: [32]and thou shalt be driven from men; and thy dwelling shall be with the beasts of the field; thou shalt be made to eat grass as oxen; and seven times shall pass over thee; until thou know that the Most High ruleth in the kingdom of men, and giveth it to whomsoever he will. [33]The same hour was the thing fulfilled upon Nebuchadnezzar: and he was driven from men, and did eat grass as oxen, and his body was wet with the dew of heaven, till his hair was grown like eagles' feathers, and his nails like birds' claws.

[34]And at the end of the days I, Nebuchadnezzar, lifted up mine eyes unto heaven, and mine understanding returned unto me, and I blessed the Most High, and I praised and honored him that liveth for ever; for his dominion is an everlasting dominion, and his kingdom from generation to generation;

[35]and all the inhabitants of the earth are reputed as nothing;
and he doeth according to his will in the army of heaven,
and among the inhabitants of the earth;
and none can stay his hand,
or say unto him, What doest thou?

[36]At the same time mine understanding returned unto me; and for the glory of my kingdom, my majesty and brightness returned unto me; and my counsellors and my lords sought unto me; and I was established in my kingdom, and excellent greatness was added unto me. [37]Now I, Nebuchadnezzar, praise and extol and honor the King of heaven; for all his works are truth, and his ways justice; and those that walk in pride he is able to abase.

Bible Study Questions and Answers

1. **Who penned Daniel 4?**

   This section of Daniel was actually written by Nebuchadnezzar. Like an open letter to his constituents, Nebuchadnezzar was addressing his kingdom.

2. **Why is the author writing the letter?**

   Nebuchadnezzar wanted to write about the miracles that God had done for him.

3. **What was the setting at the start of the letter?**

   Nebuchadnezzar was in his palace enjoying his life of leisure.

4. **Describe in detail what took place.**

   Nebuchadnezzar had a dream of a great tree that was strong and reached to heaven. A watcher, a holy one, proclaimed to have it chopped down but to keep the stump.

5. **What was the interpretation of the dream?**

   Nebuchadnezzar is to become a wild beast for seven years.

6. **What does Daniel request of Nebuchadnezzar?**

   Daniel requests Nebuchadnezzar to repent and practice righteousness.

7. **What happened in 12 months and then immediately thereafter?**

   Nebuchadnezzar was walking on the roof of the royal palace of Babylon and was extremely proud of all "his" accomplishments and wanted the glory to accompany his accomplishments. Due to his proud and boasting nature, Nebuchadnezzar was driven from his palace and placed with the beasts of the field.

8. **What did Nebuchadnezzar do that put him back in his place and how does this apply to our being cautious about striving for wealth?***

   a. Nebuchadnezzar lifted his eyes to heaven.

   b. He had everything, but it was all for his own glory. Unfortunately, God's glory shouldn't be shared since it is rightfully his. As we begin to build wealth, we need to make sure that we don't begin to place our trust in our savings.

   *Individual responses may vary.

WEALTH ACCUMULATION

QUESTION 42 ANSWERS:
ONCE WE HAVE SOME SAVINGS, HOW ARE WE TO INVEST?

Bible Study
Matthew 25:14-30

"For it is as when a man, going into another country, called his own servants, and delivered unto them his goods. [15]And unto one he gave five talents, to another two, to another one; to each according to his several ability; and he went on his journey. [16]Straightway he that received the five talents went and traded with them, and made other five talents. [17]In like manner he also that received the two gained other two. [18]But he that received the one went away and digged in the earth, and hid his lord's money."

[19]Now after a long time the lord of those servants cometh, and maketh a reckoning with them. [20]And he that received the five talents came and brought other five talents, saying, 'Lord,' thou deliveredst unto me five talents: lo, 'I have gained other five talents.'

[21]His lord said unto him, 'Well done, good and faithful servant: thou hast been faithful over a few things, I will set thee over many things; enter thou into the joy of thy lord.'

[22]And he also that received the two talents came and said, 'Lord, thou deliveredst unto me two talents: lo, I have gained other two talents.' [23]His lord said unto him, 'Well done, good and faithful servant: thou hast been faithful over a few things, I will set thee over many things; enter thou into the joy of thy lord.'

[24]And he also that had received the one talent came and said, 'Lord, I knew thee that thou art a hard man, reaping where thou didst not sow, and gathering where thou didst not scatter; [25]and I was afraid, and went away and hid thy talent in the earth: lo, thou hast thine own.' [26]But his lord answered and said unto him, 'Thou wicked and slothful servant, thou knewest that I reap where I sowed not, and gather where I did not scatter; [27]thou oughtest therefore to

have put my money to the bankers, and at my coming I should have received back mine own with interest. [28]"Take ye away therefore the talent from him, and give it unto him that hath the ten talents.'

[29]For unto every one that hath shall be given, and he shall have abundance: but from him that hath not, even that which he hath shall be taken away. [30]And cast ye out the unprofitable servant into the outer darkness: there shall be the weeping and the gnashing of teeth."

Bible Study Questions and Answers

1. Who are the characters in the Parable of the Talents taught by Jesus?

There were four characters: the master and three servants.

2. In total, how many talents did the master have?

The master began with 8 talents (5 to one servant, 2 to another, and 1 to another).

3. What percentage of his property did the master give to each servant?

    a. 5/8 or .625 or 62.5%
    b. 2/8 or .25 or 25%
    c. 1/8 or .125 or 12.5%

4. What is the reason the master gave his property to three different people?*

Although this is not specifically stated, the master divided his property to three different individuals to manage while he was gone. He could have left all his possessions to just one servant, but the master thought it best to divide amongst the servants. Again, we can only speculate why the master did this in the parable, but it seems likely that he wanted to divide the property amongst different individuals so that one person would not have control of it all.

*Individual responses may vary.

QUESTION 43 ANSWERS:
ARE WE TO BOAST ABOUT OUR INVESTMENT RETURNS?

Bible Study
Philippians 3:1-8

Finally, my brethren, rejoice in the Lord. To write the same things to you, to me indeed is not irksome, but for you it is safe. ²Beware of the dogs, beware of the evil workers, beware of the concision: ³for we are the circumcision, who worship by the Spirit of God, and glory in Christ Jesus, and have no confidence in the flesh: ⁴though I myself might have confidence even in the flesh: if any other man thinketh to have confidence in the flesh, I yet more: ⁵circumcised the eighth day, of the stock of Israel, of the tribe of Benjamin, a Hebrew of Hebrews; as touching the law, a Pharisee; ⁶as touching zeal, persecuting the church; as touching the righteousness which is in the law, found blameless. ⁷Howbeit what things were gain to me, these have I counted loss for Christ. ⁸Yea verily, and I count all things to be loss for the excellency of the knowledge of Christ Jesus my Lord: for whom I suffered the loss of all things, and do count them but refuse, that I may gain Christ,

Bible Study Questions and Answers

1. What does Paul warn us not to put our confidence in?
   Our flesh

2. What are the reasons Paul has for putting confidence in the flesh?
   a. He was circumcised on the 8th day. His family kept Jewish traditions.
   b. He was an Israelite. This connects Paul to the covenant (Abrahamic law).
   c. Paul was from the tribe of Benjamin. Few Jews actually knew the tribe they were from at that time.
   d. He was a Hebrew of Hebrews which can have at least two meanings:
      i. Paul spoke Hebrew (not all Jews did).
      ii. He had no Gentile blood in his lineage.

e. He was a Pharisee of the Law. Paul was trained under Gamaliel (a leading teacher of Jewish law during that time).

f. Paul demonstrated his zeal for God and his devotion to the Jewish customs by persecuting believers of the new "Messiah," called Jesus Christ.

3. After Paul's conversion, how did he view all the things that he could "boast" in as a Jew?

Paul counted everything as nothing for the sake of glorifying Christ.

4. What then should we be confident in; in other words, what are we able to boast about?

We are to boast only in the Lord, Jesus Christ, and him alone.

QUESTION 44 ANSWERS: CAN WE TRUST IN OUR SAVINGS AND INVESTMENTS?

Bible Study
2 Chronicles 14-16

So Abijah slept with his fathers, and they buried him in the city of David; and Asa his son reigned in his stead. In his days the land was quiet ten years. ²And Asa did that which was good and right in the eyes of Jehovah his God: ³for he took away the foreign altars, and the high places, and brake down the pillars, and hewed down the Asherim, ⁴and commanded Judah to seek Jehovah, the God of their fathers, and to do the law and the commandment. ⁵Also he took away out of all the cities of Judah the high places and the sun-images: and the kingdom was quiet before him. ⁶And he built fortified cities in Judah; for the land was quiet, and he had no war in those years, because Jehovah had given him rest. ⁷For he said unto Judah, "Let us build these cities, and make about them walls, and towers, gates, and bars; the land is yet before us, because we have sought Jehovah our God; we have sought him, and he hath given us rest on every side. So they built and prospered." ⁸And Asa had an army that bare bucklers and spears, out of Judah three hundred thousand; and out of

Benjamin, that bare shields and drew bows, two hundred and fourscore thousand: all these were mighty men of valor.

⁹And there came out against them Zerah the Ethiopian with an army of a thousand, and three hundred chariots; and he came unto Mareshah. ¹⁰Then Asa went out to meet him, and they set the battle in array in the valley of Zephathah at Mareshah. ¹¹And Asa cried unto Jehovah his God, and said, "Jehovah, there is none besides thee to help, between the mighty and him that hath no strength: help us, O Jehovah our God; for we rely on thee, and in thy name are we come against this multitude. O Jehovah, thou art our God; let not man prevail against thee." ¹²So Jehovah smote the Ethiopians before Asa, and before Judah; and the Ethiopians fled. ¹³And Asa and the people that were with him pursued them unto Gerar: and there fell of the Ethiopians so many that they could not recover themselves; for they were destroyed before Jehovah, and before his host; and they carried away very much booty. ¹⁴And they smote all the cities round about Gerar; for the fear of Jehovah came upon them: and they despoiled all the cities; for there was much spoil in them. ¹⁵They smote also the tents of cattle, and carried away sheep in abundance, and camels, and returned to Jerusalem.

¹⁵ And the Spirit of God came upon Azariah the son of Oded: ²and he went out to meet Asa, and said unto him, "Hear ye me, Asa, and all Judah and Benjamin: Jehovah is with you, while ye are with him; and if ye seek him, he will be found of you; but if ye forsake him, he will forsake you. ³Now for a long season Israel was without the true God, and without a teaching priest, and without law: ⁴but when in their distress they turned unto Jehovah, the God of Israel, and sought him, he was found of them. ⁵And in those times there was no peace to him that went out, nor to him that came in; but great vexations were upon all the inhabitants of the lands. ⁶And they were broken in pieces, nation against nation, and city against city; for God did vex them with all adversity. ⁷But be ye strong, and let not your hands be slack; for your work shall be rewarded."

⁸And when Asa heard these words, and the prophecy of Oded the prophet, he took courage, and put away the abominations out of all the land of Judah and Benjamin, and out of the cities which he had taken from the hill-country of

Ephraim; and he renewed the altar of Jehovah, that was before the porch of Jehovah. ⁹And he gathered all Judah and Benjamin, and them that sojourned with them out of Ephraim and Manasseh, and out of Simeon: for they fell to him out of Israel in abundance, when they saw that Jehovah his God was with him. ¹⁰So they gathered themselves together at Jerusalem in the third month, in the fifteenth year of the reign of Asa. ¹¹And they sacrificed unto Jehovah in that day, of the spoil which they had brought, seven hundred oxen and seven thousand sheep. ¹²And they entered into the covenant to seek Jehovah, the God of their fathers, with all their heart and with all their soul; ¹³and that whosoever would not seek Jehovah, the God of Israel, should be put to death, whether small or great, whether man or woman. ¹⁴And they sware unto Jehovah with a loud voice, and with shouting, and with trumpets, and with cornets. ¹⁵And all Judah rejoiced at the oath; for they had sworn with all their heart, and sought him with their whole desire; and he was found of them: and Jehovah gave them rest round about.

¹⁶And also Maacah, the mother of Asa the king, he removed from being queen, because she had made an abominable image for an Asherah; and Asa cut down her image, and made dust of it, and burnt it at the brook Kidron. ¹⁷But the high places were not taken away out of Israel: nevertheless the heart of Asa was perfect all his days. ¹⁸And he brought into the house of God the things that his father had dedicated, and that he himself had dedicated, silver, and gold, and vessels. ¹⁹And there was no more war unto the five and thirtieth year of the reign of Asa.

¹⁶ In the six and thirtieth year of the reign of Asa, Baasha king of Israel went up against Judah, and built Ramah, that he might not suffer any one to go out or come in to Asa king of Judah. ²Then Asa brought out silver and gold out of the treasures of the house of Jehovah and of the king's house, and sent to Ben-hadad king of Syria, that dwelt at Damascus, saying, ³There is a league between me and thee, as there was between my father and thy father: behold, I have sent thee silver and gold; go, break thy league with Baasha king of Israel, that he may depart from me. ⁴And Ben-hadad hearkened unto king Asa, and sent the captains of his armies against the cities of Israel; and they smote Ijon, and Dan, and Abel-maim, and all the store-cities of Naphtali. ⁵And it came to pass, when Baasha heard thereof, that he left off building Ramah, and

let his work cease. ⁶Then Asa the king took all Judah; and they carried away the stones of Ramah, and the timber thereof, wherewith Baasha had builded; and he built therewith Geba and Mizpah.

⁷And at that time Hanani the seer came to Asa king of Judah, and said unto him, "Because thou hast relied on the king of Syria, and hast not relied on Jehovah thy God, therefore is the host of the king of Syria escaped out of thy hand. ⁸Were not the Ethiopians and the Lubim a huge host, with chariots and horsemen exceeding many? yet, because thou didst rely on Jehovah, he delivered them into thy hand. ⁹For the eyes of Jehovah run to and fro throughout the whole earth, to show himself strong in the behalf of them whose heart is perfect toward him. Herein thou hast done foolishly; for from henceforth thou shalt have wars." ¹⁰Then Asa was wroth with the seer, and put him in the prison-house; for he was in a rage with him because of this thing. And Asa oppressed some of the people at the same time.

¹¹And, behold, the acts of Asa, first and last, lo, they are written in the book of the kings of Judah and Israel. ¹²And in the thirty and ninth year of his reign Asa was diseased in his feet; his disease was exceeding great: yet in his disease he sought not to Jehovah, but to the physicians. ¹³And Asa slept with his fathers, and died in the one and fortieth year of his reign. ¹⁴And they buried him in his own sepulchres, which he had hewn out for himself in the city of David, and laid him in the bed which was filled with sweet odors and divers kinds of spices prepared by the perfumers' art: and they made a very great burning for him.

Bible Study Questions and Answers

1. After 10 years of Asa's reign, who came out to start a war with Judah?

   Zerah, the Ethiopian, came out to war with an army of a million men and 300 chariots.

2. What was Asa's first response when he went out to meet Zerah's army?

   Asa cried out to the Lord his God!

3. **What was the outcome of the battle?**

   The Lord defeated the Ethiopians, and the men of Judah carried away a vast amount of spoils from their victory.

4. **In 2 Chronicles 15, what did Azariah tell Asa?**

   Azriah tells Asa that he will be with the Lord, the Lord will be with him, but if he abandons the Lord, the Lord will abandon him.

5. **What event occurred in the 36ᵗʰ year of Asa's reign?**

   Israel began to build at Ramah to cut off supplies to Judah.

6. **What did Asa do in response to the building of Ramah?**

   Asa sent money from the treasury of the House of the Lord to Ben-hadad, King of Syria and desired a covenant with him. The covenant was to stop Baasha, King of Israel, from building at Ramah.

7. **Did Asa's strategy work? Explain.**

   Yes, Baasha stopped building at Ramah and let his work cease.

8. **What happened in response to Asa placing trust in the covenant made with Ben-hadad instead of Jehovah?**

   Asa lost the support of the King of Syria.

9. **Why do you think that Asa did not seek God in the second crisis?***

   Asa may not have thought the second crisis was worthy of God's provision or Asa felt that he had enough silver and gold in the treasury of the house of the Lord to provide protection. Asa may have wrongly presumed that he had the provision to protect his people, so why would he need to rely on God?

   *Individual responses may vary.

QUESTION 45 ANSWERS:
WHAT ARE WE TO DO WITH THE WEALTH WE CREATE FROM OUR INVESTMENTS?

Bible Study
Numbers 18:8–32 and Deuteronomy 14:22–29

Numbers 18:8–32

And Jehovah spake unto Aaron, "And I, behold, I have given thee the charge of my heave-offerings, even all the hallowed things of the children of Israel; unto thee have I given them by reason of the anointing, and to thy sons, as a portion for ever. ⁹This shall be thine of the most holy things, reserved from the fire: every oblation of theirs, even every meal-offering of theirs, and every sin-offering of theirs, and every trespass-offering of theirs, which they shall render unto me, shall be most holy for thee and for thy sons. ¹⁰As the most holy things shalt thou eat thereof; every male shall eat thereof: it shall be holy unto thee. ¹¹And this is thine: the heave-offering of their gift, even all the wave-offerings of the children of Israel; I have given them unto thee, and to thy sons and to thy daughters with thee, as a portion for ever; every one that is clean in thy house shall eat thereof. ¹²All the best of the oil, and all the best of the vintage, and of the grain, the firstfruits of them which they give unto Jehovah, to thee have I given them. ¹³The first-ripe fruits of all that is in their land, which they bring unto Jehovah, shall be thine; every one that is clean in thy house shall eat thereof. ¹⁴Every thing devoted in Israel shall be thine. ¹⁵Every thing that openeth the womb, of all flesh which they offer unto Jehovah, both of man and beast shall be thine: nevertheless the firstborn of man shalt thou surely redeem, and the firstling of unclean beasts shalt thou redeem. ¹⁶And those that are to be redeemed of them from a month old shalt thou redeem, according to thine estimation, for the money of five shekels, after the shekel of the sanctuary (the same is twenty gerahs). ¹⁷But the firstling of a cow, or the firstling of a sheep, or the firstling of a goat, thou shalt not redeem; they are holy: thou shalt sprinkle their blood upon the altar, and shalt burn their fat for an offering made by fire, for a sweet savor unto Jehovah. ¹⁸And the flesh of them shall be thine, as the wave-breast and as the right thigh, it shall be thine."

¹⁹All the heave-offerings of the holy things, which the children of Israel offer unto Jehovah, have I given thee, and thy sons and thy daughters with thee, as a portion for ever: it is a covenant of salt for ever before Jehovah unto thee and to thy seed with thee. ²⁰And Jehovah said unto Aaron, "Thou shalt have no inheritance in their land, neither shalt thou have any portion among them: I am thy portion and thine inheritance among the children of Israel.

²¹And unto the children of Levi, behold, I have given all the tithe in Israel for an inheritance, in return for their service which they serve, even the service of the tent of meeting. ²²And henceforth the children of Israel shall not come nigh the tent of meeting, lest they bear sin, and die. ²³But the Levites shall do the service of the tent of meeting, and they shall bear their iniquity: it shall be a statute for ever throughout your generations; and among the children of Israel they shall have no inheritance. ²⁴For the tithe of the children of Israel, which they offer as a heave-offering unto Jehovah, I have given to the Levites for an inheritance: therefore I have said unto them, 'Among the children of Israel they shall have no inheritance.'"

²⁵And Jehovah spake unto Moses, saying, ²⁶"Moreover thou shalt speak unto the Levites, and say unto them, 'When ye take of the children of Israel the tithe which I have given you from them for your inheritance, then ye shall offer up a heave-offering of it for Jehovah, a tithe of the tithe. ²⁷And your heave-offering shall be reckoned unto you, as though it were the grain of the threshing-floor, and as the fulness of the winepress. ²⁸Thus ye also shall offer a heave-offering unto Jehovah of all your tithes, which ye receive of the children of Israel; and thereof ye shall give Jehovah's heave-offering to Aaron the priest. ²⁹Out of all your gifts ye shall offer every heave-offering of Jehovah, of all the best thereof, even the hallowed part thereof out of it.'" ³⁰"Therefore thou shalt say unto them, 'When ye heave the best thereof from it, then it shall be reckoned unto the Levites as the increase of the threshing-floor, and as the increase of the winepress. ³¹And ye shall eat it in every place, ye and your households: for it is your reward in return for your service in the tent of meeting. ³²And ye shall bear no sin by reason of it, when ye have heaved from it the best thereof: and ye shall not profane the holy things of the children of Israel, that ye die not.'"

Deuteronomy 14:22–29

Thou shalt surely tithe all the increase of thy seed, that which cometh forth from the field year by year. [23]And thou shalt eat before Jehovah thy God, in the place which he shall choose, to cause his name to dwell there, the tithe of thy grain, of thy new wine, and of thine oil, and the firstlings of thy herd and of thy flock; that thou mayest learn to fear Jehovah thy God always. [24]And if the way be too long for thee, so that thou art not able to carry it, because the place is too far from thee, which Jehovah thy God shall choose, to set his name there, when Jehovah thy God shall bless thee; [25]then shalt thou turn it into money, and bind up the money in thy hand, and shalt go unto the place which Jehovah thy God shall choose: [26]and thou shalt bestow the money for whatsoever thy soul desireth, for oxen, or for sheep, or for wine, or for strong drink, or for whatsoever thy soul asketh of thee; and thou shalt eat there before Jehovah thy God, and thou shalt rejoice, thou and thy household. [27]And the Levite that is within thy gates, thou shalt not forsake him; for he hath no portion nor inheritance with thee. [28]At the end of every three years thou shalt bring forth all the tithe of thine increase in the same year, and shalt lay it up within thy gates: [29]and the Levite, because he hath no portion nor inheritance with thee, and the sojourner, and the fatherless, and the widow, that are within thy gates, shall come, and shall eat and be satisfied; that Jehovah thy God may bless thee in all the work of thy hand which thou doest.

Bible Study Questions and Answers

1. According to Numbers 18, what were the Israelites commanded to support?

   The Israelites were to give towards the support of full-time religious workers who were not given land of their own.

2. What were the Israelites to support with their resources, according to Deuteronomy 14:22–27?

   They were to give resources for community meals to celebrate religious fellowships.

3. How often were the two offerings required?

The two offerings were required once a year.

4. Review Deuteronomy 14:28–29. What were the Israelites supposed to support and how often?

The Israelites were to support the needs of the poor once every three years.

5. How much was each of the three offerings supposed to be?

A tenth (1/10th)

6. What were the Israelites to do with the remaining portion of their resources?*

The Israelites were to provide for their family through consumption of their crops and livestock and or sell these items to buy other life's necessities.

*Individual responses may vary.

BORROWING AND LENDING

QUESTION 46 ANSWERS:
WHAT EXPECTATIONS SHOULD WE HAVE WHEN
WE LEND TO SOMEONE?

Bible Study
Deuteronomy 15:1–11

At the end of every seven years thou shalt make a release. ²And this is the manner of the release: every creditor shall release that which he hath lent unto his neighbor; he shall not exact it of his neighbor and his brother; because Jehovah's release hath been proclaimed. ³Of a foreigner thou mayest exact it: but whatsoever of thine is with thy brother thy hand shall release. ⁴Howbeit there shall be no poor with thee (for Jehovah will surely bless thee in the land which Jehovah thy God giveth thee for an inheritance to possess it), ⁵if only thou diligently hearken unto the voice of Jehovah thy God, to observe to do all this commandment which I command thee this day. ⁶For Jehovah thy God will bless thee, as he promised thee: and thou shalt lend unto many nations, but thou shalt not borrow; and thou shalt rule over many nations, but they shall not rule over thee.

⁷If there be with thee a poor man, one of thy brethren, within any of thy gates in thy land which Jehovah thy God giveth thee, thou shalt not harden thy heart, nor shut thy hand from thy poor brother; ⁸but thou shalt surely open thy hand unto him, and shalt surely lend him sufficient for his need in that which he wanteth. ⁹Beware that there be not a base thought in thy heart, saying, "The seventh year, the year of release, is at hand; and thine eye be evil against thy poor brother, and thou give him nought; and he cry unto Jehovah against thee, and it be sin unto thee." ¹⁰Thou shalt surely give him, and thy heart shall not be grieved when thou givest unto him; because that for this thing Jehovah thy God will bless thee in all thy work, and in all that thou puttest thy hand unto. ¹¹For the poor will never cease out of the land: therefore I command thee, saying, Thou shalt surely open thy hand unto thy brother, to thy needy, and to thy poor, in thy land.

Bible Study Questions and Answers

1. What were the Israelites supposed to do every seven years with other Israelites who owed them money?

   The debts were to be cancelled.

2. How were the Israelites to handle the poor among them?

   They were not to be hardhearted or tightfisted toward them, but rather be openhanded and freely lend them whatever they need.

3. What did Moses caution the Israelites about concerning the 7th Year debt cancellation?

   They were not to show ill will toward their fellow Israelites by not lending to them when realizing they would not receive anything in return.

4. According to Moses, what was to be the Israelites' attitude toward giving?

   Th Israelites were to give generously to them and to do so without a grudging heart. The Lord will then bless them in all their work and in everything they put their hand to.

5. How does our attitude toward giving relate to not expecting anything in return when we lend to others?*

   We need to be mindful of our attitude toward the possessions God has entrusted to us. As a steward, one who does not "own" anything but merely manages God's resources, when we lend or when we give, we are merely transferring the ownership to another steward! This concept is why lending and giving should be viewed in the same manner.

   *Individual responses may vary.

QUESTION 47 ANSWERS:
IS IT OKAY TO BORROW MONEY?

Bible Study
Haggai 1–2

In the second year of Darius the king, in the sixth month, in the first day of the month, came the word of Jehovah by Haggai the prophet unto Zerubbabel the son of Shealtiel, governor of Judah, and to Joshua the son of Jehozadak, the high priest, saying, ² Thus speaketh Jehovah of hosts, saying, "This people say, 'It is not the time for us to come, the time for Jehovah's house to be built.'" ³ Then came the word of Jehovah by Haggai the prophet, saying, ⁴ "Is it a time for you yourselves to dwell in your ceiled houses, while this house lieth waste? ⁵ Now therefore thus saith Jehovah of hosts: 'Consider your ways.' ⁶ Ye have sown much, and bring in little; ye eat, but ye have not enough; ye drink, but ye are not filled with drink; ye clothe you, but there is none warm; and he that earneth wages earneth wages to put it into a bag with holes.'"

⁷ "Thus saith Jehovah of hosts: 'Consider your ways. ⁸ Go up to the mountain, and bring wood, and build the house; and I will take pleasure in it, and I will be glorified,' saith Jehovah. ⁹ Ye looked for much, and, lo, it came to little; and when ye brought it home, I did blow upon it. 'Why?' saith Jehovah of hosts. 'Because of my house that lieth waste, while ye run every man to his own house. ¹⁰ Therefore for your sake the heavens withhold the dew, and the earth withholdeth its fruit. ¹¹ And I called for a drought upon the land, and upon the mountains, and upon the grain, and upon the new wine, and upon the oil, and upon that which the ground bringeth forth, and upon men, and upon cattle, and upon all the labor of the hands.'"

¹² Then Zerubbabel the son of Shealtiel, and Joshua the son of Jehozadak, the high priest, with all the remnant of the people, obeyed the voice of Jehovah their God, and the words of Haggai the prophet, as Jehovah their God had sent him; and the people did fear before Jehovah. ¹³ Then spake Haggai Jehovah's messenger in Jehovah's message unto the people, saying, "'I am with you,' saith Jehovah." ¹⁴ And Jehovah stirred up the spirit of Zerubbabel the son of Shealtiel, governor of Judah, and the spirit of Joshua the son of

Jehozadak, the high priest, and the spirit of all the remnant of the people; and they came and did work on the house of Jehovah of hosts, their God, [15] in the four and twentieth day of the month, in the sixth month, in the second year of Darius the king.

[2] In the seventh month, in the one and twentieth day of the month, came the word of Jehovah by Haggai the prophet, saying, [2] "Speak now to Zerubbabel the son of Shealtiel, governor of Judah, and to Joshua the son of Jehozadak, the high priest, and to the remnant of the people, saying, [3] 'Who is left among you that saw this house in its former glory? and how do ye see it now? is it not in your eyes as nothing? [4] Yet now be strong, O Zerubbabel, saith Jehovah; and be strong, O Joshua, son of Jehozadak, the high priest; and be strong, all ye people of the land, saith Jehovah, and work: for I am with you, saith Jehovah of hosts, [5] according to the word that I covenanted with you when ye came out of Egypt, and my Spirit abode among you: fear ye not.' [6] For thus saith Jehovah of hosts: 'Yet once, it is a little while, and I will shake the heavens, and the earth, and the sea, and the dry land; [7] and I will shake all nations; and the precious things of all nations shall come; and I will fill this house with glory, saith Jehovah of hosts. [8] The silver is mine, and the gold is mine,' saith Jehovah of hosts. [9] 'The latter glory of this house shall be greater than the former,' saith Jehovah of hosts; 'and in this place will I give peace, saith Jehovah of hosts.'"

[10] In the four and twentieth day of the ninth month, in the second year of Darius, came the word of Jehovah by Haggai the prophet, saying, [11] "Thus saith Jehovah of hosts: 'Ask now the priests concerning the law, saying, [12] If one bear holy flesh in the skirt of his garment, and with his skirt do touch bread, or pottage, or wine, or oil, or any food, shall it become holy?'" And the priests answered and said, No. [13] Then said Haggai, "If one that is unclean by reason of a dead body touch any of these, shall it be unclean?" And the priests answered and said, "It shall be unclean." [14] Then answered Haggai and said, "'So is this people, and so is this nation before me,' saith Jehovah; 'and so is every work of their hands; and that which they offer there is unclean.'[15] And now, I pray you, consider from this day and backward, before a stone was laid upon a stone in the temple of Jehovah. [16] Through all that time, when one came to a heap of twenty measures, there were but ten; when one came to

the winevat to draw out fifty vessels, there were but twenty. ¹⁷ I smote you with blasting and with mildew and with hail in all the work of your hands; yet ye turned not to me,' saith Jehovah. ¹⁸ 'Consider, I pray you, from this day and backward, from the four and twentieth day of the ninth month, since the day that the foundation of Jehovah's temple was laid, consider it. ¹⁹ Is the seed yet in the barn? yea, the vine, and the fig-tree, and the pomegranate, and the olive-tree have not brought forth; from this day will I bless you."

²⁰ And the word of Jehovah came the second time unto Haggai in the four and twentieth day of the month, saying, ²¹ "'Speak to Zerubbabel, governor of Judah, saying, 'I will shake the heavens and the earth; ²² and I will overthrow the throne of kingdoms; and I will destroy the strength of the kingdoms of the nations; and I will overthrow the chariots, and those that ride in them; and the horses and their riders shall come down, every one by the sword of his brother. ²³ In that day, saith Jehovah of hosts, will I take thee, O Zerubbabel, my servant, the son of Shealtiel, saith Jehovah, and will make thee as a signet; for I have chosen thee, saith Jehovah of hosts.'"

Bible Study Questions and Answers

1. What was the first thing that the prophet Haggai told to Zerubbabel and Joshua?

    The Israelites were saying that it wasn't time to rebuild the house of the Lord.

2. What question did Haggai then pose to the people of Israel?

    Haggai poses to the Israelites a rhetorical question, "Should you live in very nice houses while the Lord's house remains in disarray?"

3. What were the outcomes of the Israelites' focus on themselves?
    a. Little was harvested from their fields.
    b. They would eat but never be filled.
    c. They would drink but their thirst would not be quenched.
    d. Their clothes would never keep them warm.
    e. They would earn money but they would not be able to save.

4. What should the Israelites have focused on instead of their own possessions?

> The Israelites should have focused on the House of the Lord before worrying about their own homes.

5. What did the Lord declare through Haggai once the people accepted his message?

> The Lord tells Haggai that he is with them.

6. How many times does the word "consider" occur in the book of Haggai?
    a. Chapter 1—Two times
    b. Chapter 2—Three times

7. What is the reason for such a strong emphasis?*

> In the two chapters of Haggai, we see a recurring warning to the people. Taking place a total of five times, the repeated cautionary word, "consider" is quite significant—for, as people of God, we are to consider our ways and seek to put God first.

*Individual responses may vary.

QUESTION 48 ANSWERS:
WHAT ARE OUR RESPONSIBILITIES IF WE BORROW MONEY?

Bible Study
James 4:13-17

Come now, ye that say, today or tomorrow we will go into this city, and spend a year there, and trade, and get gain: [14] whereas ye know not what shall be on the morrow. What is your life? For ye are a vapor that appeareth for a little time, and then vanisheth away. [15] For that ye ought to say, If the Lord will, we shall both live, and do this or that. [16] But now ye glory in your vauntings: all such glorying is evil. [17] To him therefore that knoweth to do good, and doeth it not, to him it is sin.

Bible Study Questions and Answers

1. Who was James talking to?

   James is talking to those people who desire to go and make money.

2. What questions does James pose to the people?

   James asked his audience to reflect on why they were desiring money and to consider what was important in their lives.

3. The questions James asked may be rhetorical, but he provides his reasons for asking. What reasons were given to the people?

   James tells the people that they do not know what will happen in the future, and that each person's life is like a "vapor" that is seen only for a moment and then disappears.

4. What does James say we should do?

   James instructs us to first seek the will of the Lord and then to do the Lord's will.

5. What does James say we do that is evil?

   We boast in our arrogant schemes.

6. How does our evil boasting relate back to our paying debts?*

   For many of us, when borrowing money, we are given a payment schedule that is based on the idea we will go somewhere (e.g., a city, market, organization) to make money today and the following tomorrows. James acknowledges that we are fragile, a vapor, and do not know what will happen one day to the next. Yet, when we are employed, our tendency is to think we will continue to have the ability to make the monthly payment (which may be looked at as our 'arrogant schemes'). James reminds us that our dependence always needs to be firmly established in Christ and his will.

   *Individual responses may vary.

GREED

QUESTION 49 ANSWERS:
WHAT IS GREED?

Bible Study
1 Kings 21

And it came to pass after these things, that Naboth the Jezreelite had a vine-yard, which was in Jezreel, hard by the palace of Ahab king of Samaria. ²And Ahab spake unto Naboth, saying, "Give me thy vineyard, that I may have it for a garden of herbs, because it is near unto my house; and I will give thee for it a better vineyard than it: or, if it seem good to thee, I will give thee the worth of it in money." ³And Naboth said to Ahab, "Jehovah forbid it me, that I should give the inheritance of my fathers unto thee." ⁴And Ahab came into his house heavy and displeased because of the word which Naboth the Jezreelite had spoken to him; for he had said, "I will not give thee the inheritance of my fathers." And he laid him down upon his bed, and turned away his face, and would eat no bread.

⁵But Jezebel his wife came to him, and said unto him, "Why is thy spirit so sad, that thou eatest no bread?" ⁶And he said unto her, Because I spake unto Naboth the Jezreelite, and said unto him, "Give me thy vineyard for money; or else, if it please thee, I will give thee another vineyard for it: and he answered, I will not give thee my vineyard." ⁷And Jezebel his wife said unto him, "Dost thou now govern the kingdom of Israel? arise, and eat bread, and let thy heart be merry: I will give thee the vineyard of Naboth the Jezreelite." ⁸So she wrote letters in Ahab's name, and sealed them with his seal, and sent the letters unto the elders and to the nobles that were in his city, and that dwelt with Naboth. ⁹And she wrote in the letters, saying, "Proclaim a fast, and set Naboth on high among the people: ¹⁰and set two men, base fellows, before him, and let them bear witness against him, saying, 'Thou didst curse God and the king.' And then carry him out, and stone him to death."

¹¹And the men of his city, even the elders and the nobles who dwelt in his city, did as Jezebel had sent unto them, according as it was written in the letters

which she had sent unto them. ¹²They proclaimed a fast, and set Naboth on high among the people. ¹³And the two men, the base fellows, came in and sat before him: and the base fellows bare witness against him, even against Naboth, in the presence of the people, saying, "Naboth did curse God and the king." Then they carried him forth out of the city, and stoned him to death with stones. ¹⁴Then they sent to Jezebel, saying, "Naboth is stoned, and is dead." ¹⁵And it came to pass, when Jezebel heard that Naboth was stoned, and was dead, that Jezebel said to Ahab, "Arise, take possession of the vineyard of Naboth the Jezreelite, which he refused to give thee for money; for Naboth is not alive, but dead." ¹⁶And it came to pass, when Ahab heard that Naboth was dead, that Ahab rose up to go down to the vineyard of Naboth the Jezreelite, to take possession of it.

¹⁷And the word of Jehovah came to Elijah the Tishbite, saying, ¹⁸"Arise, go down to meet Ahab king of Israel, who dwelleth in Samaria: behold, he is in the vineyard of Naboth, whither he is gone down to take possession of it. ¹⁹And thou shalt speak unto him, saying, 'Thus saith Jehovah, Hast thou killed and also taken possession?' And thou shalt speak unto him, saying, 'Thus saith Jehovah, In the place where dogs licked the blood of Naboth shall dogs lick thy blood, even thine.'" ²⁰And Ahab said to Elijah, "Hast thou found me, O mine enemy?" And he answered, "I have found thee, because thou hast sold thyself to do that which is evil in the sight of Jehovah. ²¹Behold, I will bring evil upon thee, and will utterly sweep thee away and will cut off from Ahab every man-child, and him that is shut up and him that is left at large in Israel: ²²and I will make thy house like the house of Jeroboam the son of Nebat, and like the house of Baasha the son of Ahijah for the provocation wherewith thou hast provoked me to anger, and hast made Israel to sin." ²³"And of Jezebel also spake Jehovah, saying, 'The dogs shall eat Jezebel by the rampart of Jezreel. ²⁴Him that dieth of Ahab in the city the dogs shall eat; and him that dieth in the field shall the birds of the heavens eat.'" ²⁵(But there was none like unto Ahab, who did sell himself to do that which was evil in the sight of Jehovah, whom Jezebel his wife stirred up. ²⁶And he did very abominably in following idols, according to all that the Amorites did, whom Jehovah cast out before the children of Israel.)

[27]And it came to pass, when Ahab heard those words, that he rent his clothes, and put sackcloth upon his flesh, and fasted, and lay in sackcloth, and went softly. [28]And the word of Jehovah came to Elijah the Tishbite, saying, [29]"Seest thou how Ahab humbleth himself before me? because he humbleth himself before me, I will not bring the evil in his days; but in his son's days will I bring the evil upon his house."

Bible Study Questions and Answers

1. **What did Ahab want that was close to his palace?**
   Ahab wanted a vineyard that was owned by Naboth, a Jezreelite.

2. **What did Ahab offer Naboth?**
   Ahab offered to give Naboth a better vineyard or pay him the value of the vineyard.

3. **What was Naboth's response?**
   Naboth did not part with the vineyard because God forbid him to give up the inheritance of his ancestors.

4. **How did Ahab respond to Naboth?**
   Ahab went home sullen and angry, and laid down on his bed sulking and refusing to eat. In other words, he was throwing a tantrum.

5. **What happened when Ahab told his wife, Jezebel, about his dealings with Naboth?**
   Jezebel, using the King's seal, ordered to have Naboth charged with blasphemy and stoned to death.

6. **What did Elijah say to Ahab when he met Ahab at Naboth's vineyard?**
   Elijah tells Ahab that because he sinned against the Lord, the Lord will eliminate his descendants and cut Ahab off from Israel.

7. **After looking at this scenario, what can greed do in our lives?***
   Greed can make us act in ways that go against our Lord and Savior. Just as Luke reminds us—we need to be on the look-out for all kinds of covetousness (greed) since our life does not

depend on our possessions. If we are not careful, we may set up idols in our life by continually desiring more and more for ourselves. God gives us exactly what we need.

Individual responses may vary.

QUESTION 50 ANSWERS:
WHAT ARE THE CONSEQUENCES OF GREED?

Bible Study
Colossians 3:1-6

If then ye were raised together with Christ, seek the things that are above, where Christ is, seated on the right hand of God. [2]Set your mind on the things that are above, not on the things that are upon the earth. [3]For ye died, and your life is hid with Christ in God. [4]When Christ, who is our life, shall be manifested, then shall ye also with him be manifested in glory.

[5]Put to death therefore your members which are upon the earth: fornication, uncleanness, passion, evil desire, and covetousness, which is idolatry; [6]for which things' sake cometh the wrath of God upon the sons of disobedience:

Bible Study Questions

1. What does Paul instruct those in Colossae since they have been raised in Christ?

   To set their hearts on things above, where Christ is seated at the right hand of God.

2. In addition to our hearts, what else are we to set on things above? Why?

   We are to set out mind on things above and not on earthly things. For we have died and our life is now hidden with Christ in God, and when Christ appears in Glory, we will appear with him.

3. What advice does Paul give to the church in Colossae?

   The people were instructed by Paul to put to death whatever belonged to their earthly nature, including evil desires and greed.

4. **What does Paul call earthly-natured behaviors?**

Paul refers to earthly-natured behaviors as idolatry.

5. **What reason does Paul give for why we should give up earthly-natured behaviors?**

The reason we should give up earthly-natured behaviors, such as evil desires and greed, is because God's wrath is coming.

6. **What impact does Paul's words have on you?***

In our culture, it is hard for us to consider too much of anything as being a bad thing. The desire to always have more seems to be a "part of us." However, we need to carefully consider who we serve and that what we have is not our own, but the Lord's.

*Individual responses may vary.

QUESTION 51 ANSWERS:
WHAT DOES GREED LEAD TO IN OUR SPIRITUAL LIVES?

Bible Study
Ezekiel 14:1-8

Then came certain of the elders of Israel unto me, and sat before me. ²And the word of Jehovah came unto me, saying, ³Son of man, these men have taken their idols into their heart, and put the stumblingblock of their iniquity before their face: should I be inquired of at all by them? ⁴Therefore speak unto them, and say unto them, 'Thus saith the Lord Jehovah: Every man of the house of Israel that taketh his idols into his heart, and putteth the stumblingblock of his iniquity before his face, and cometh to the prophet; I Jehovah will answer him therein according to the multitude of his idols; ⁵that I may take the house of Israel in their own heart, because they are all estranged from me through their idols.'"

⁶"Therefore say unto the house of Israel, 'Thus saith the Lord Jehovah: Return ye, and turn yourselves from your idols; and turn away your faces from all

your abominations. [7]For every one of the house of Israel, or of the strangers that sojourn in Israel, that separateth himself from me, and taketh his idols into his heart, and putteth the stumblingblock of his iniquity before his face, and cometh to the prophet to inquire for himself of me; I Jehovah will answer him by myself: [8]and I will set my face against that man, and will make him an astonishment, for a sign and a proverb, and I will cut him off from the midst of my people; and ye shall know that I am Jehovah.'"

Bible Study Questions and Answers

1. What response did God give to the Priest/Prophet Ezekiel when some of the elders came to inquire of him?

   The Lord spoke to Ezekiel and informed him that some men have established idols in their life and that this wickedness has created barriers before their faces.

2. What did God tell Ezekiel he would do to the Israelites who were idolizers?

   God told Ezekiel that he would address the idolizers himself.

3. What was Ezekiel instructed to tell the people of Israel?

   They were told to repent and turn away from their idols, and renounce all of their detestable practices.

4. What happened if any Israelite or foreigner inquired of a prophet with idols in their hearts?

   Idolatry is estrangement from God and so those with idols in their hearts were to be removed (estranged) from the House of Israel (God's people).

5. How does God's response to idolization inform us about his character toward greed?*

   Idolatry is probably one of the biggest abominations to the Lord. We are told to have no other god before the Lord our God (Ex. 20:2) and to love him with all our heart, soul and, mind (Matt. 22:37).

*Individual responses may vary.

SUPPLEMENTAL QUESTION 1 ANSWERS: IF MONEY IS SO IMPORTANT TO GOD, HOW DO WE GET HELP?

Bible Study
2 Chronicles 1

And Solomon the son of David was strengthened in his kingdom, and Jehovah his God was with him, and magnified him exceedingly. ²And Solomon spake unto all Israel, to the captains of thousands and of hundreds, and to the judges, and to every prince in all Israel, the heads of the fathers' houses. ³So Solomon, and all the assembly with him, went to the high place that was at Gibeon; for there was the tent of meeting of God, which Moses the servant of Jehovah had made in the wilderness. ⁴But the ark of God had David brought up from Kiriath-jearim to the place that David had prepared for it; for he had pitched a tent for it at Jerusalem. ⁵Moreover the brazen altar, that Bezalel the son of Uri, the son of Hur, had made, was there before the tabernacle of Jehovah: and Solomon and the assembly sought unto it. ⁶And Solomon went up thither to the brazen altar before Jehovah, which was at the tent of meeting, and offered a thousand burnt-offerings upon it.

⁷In that night did God appear unto Solomon, and said unto him, "Ask what I shall give thee." ⁸And Solomon said unto God, "Thou hast showed great lovingkindness unto David my father, and hast made me king in his stead. ⁹Now, O Jehovah God, let thy promise unto David my father be established; for thou hast made me king over a people like the dust of the earth in multitude. ¹⁰Give me now wisdom and knowledge, that I may go out and come in before this people; for who can judge this thy people, that is so great?" ¹¹And God said to Solomon, "Because this was in thy heart, and thou hast not asked riches, wealth, or honor, nor the life of them that hate thee, neither yet hast asked long life; but hast asked wisdom and knowledge for thyself, that thou mayest judge my people, over whom I have made thee king: ¹²wisdom and knowledge is granted unto thee; and I will give thee riches, and wealth, and honor, such as none of the kings have had that have been before thee; neither shall there any after thee have the like." ¹³So Solomon came from the high place that was at Gibeon, from before the tent of meeting, unto Jerusalem; and he reigned over Israel.

¹⁴And Solomon gathered chariots and horsemen: and he had a thousand and four hundred chariots, and twelve thousand horsemen, that he placed in the chariot cities, and with the king at Jerusalem. ¹⁵And the king made silver and gold to be in Jerusalem as stones, and cedars made he to be as the Sycamore trees that are in the lowland, for abundance. ¹⁶And the horses which Solomon had were brought out of Egypt; the king's merchants received them in droves, each drove at a price. ¹⁷And they fetched up and brought out of Egypt a chariot for six hundred shekels of silver, and a horse for a hundred and fifty: and so for all the kings of the Hittites, and the kings of Syria, did they bring them out by their means.

Bible Study Questions and Answers

1. How does 2 Chronicles begin?

   Solomon established himself in his kingdom and the Lord his God was with him and made him exceedingly great.

2. As Solomon offered burnt offerings at the bronze altar in the tent of meeting, what happened?

   God appeared to Solomon and asked him what God should give to him.

3. What did Solomon reply?

   Solomon asked for wisdom and knowledge so that he could rule God's people.

4. How did God respond?

   God was pleased that Solomon asked for wisdom and knowledge over wealth, possessions, or longer life that he granted Solomon's request.

5. What else does God give to Solomon?

   God also gave Solomon riches, possessions, and honor, such as none of the kings had who were before Solomon and none after Solomon shall have such riches, possessions, and honor.

6. What makes this request so pleasing to God?*

   We serve a loving God and he wants us to bear his image and be Christlike, fulfilling and acting with love toward others. When Solomon asked for wisdom and knowledge, he did so out of love for God and his people. It was not a selfish request. Solomon also knew that he could not manage the responsibility on his own; he needed God's guidance.

*Individual responses may vary.

SUPPLEMENTAL QUESTION 2 ANSWERS: HOW SHOULD WE SEEK BIBLICAL COUNSEL?

Bible Study
1 Kings 2:1-4 and Proverbs 1:8-9; 6:20-22; 23:22

1 Kings 2:1-4

Now the days of David drew nigh that he should die; and he charged Solomon his son, saying, ²"I am going the way of all the earth: be thou strong therefore, and show thyself a man; ³and keep the charge of Jehovah thy God, to walk in his ways, to keep his statutes, and his commandments, and his ordinances, and his testimonies, according to that which is written in the law of Moses, that thou mayest prosper in all that thou doest, and whithersoever thou turnest thyself; ⁴that Jehovah may establish his word which he spake concerning me, saying, If thy children take heed to their way, to walk before me in truth with all their heart and with all their soul, there shall not fail thee (said he) a man on the throne of Israel."

Proverbs 1:8-9

My son, hear the instruction of thy father, And forsake not the law of thy mother: ⁹For they shall be a chaplet of grace unto thy head, And chains about thy neck.

Proverbs 6:20-22

My son, keep the commandment of thy father, And forsake not the law of thy mother: ²¹Bind them continually upon thy heart; Tie them about thy neck. ²²When thou walkest, it shall lead thee; When thou sleepest, it shall watch over thee; And when thou awakest, it shall talk with thee.

Proverbs 23:22
Hearken unto thy father that begat thee, And despise not thy mother when she is old.

Bible Study Questions and Answers

1. What are some of the qualifications that make parents a great resource for biblical counsel?

    They have more knowledge, in many cases, and far more life experiences in which to provide.

2. According to Proverbs 6:20–22, what will your father's and mother's instruction do for you?

    They will guide you, watch over you, and talk to you.

3. What sound counsel did David give to Solomon on his deathbed?

    That Solomon should keep the charge of the Lord your God, walk in his ways, keep his statutes, keep his commandments, keep his ordinances, and keep his testimonies

4. How can you and your family set up a method of communication such that the children can seek openly the counsel of the parents?*

    There is no specific answer here. As a family, talk through the various ways to open up communications (e.g., weekly sit-down meetings, family dinner conversations, etc.) so that the children know they can turn to you for advice, specifically as it relates to managing money.

    Use the "Family Meeting Agenda" in the Appendix as a guide in your family meetings.

    *Individual responses may vary.

CPSIA information can be obtained
at www.ICGtesting.com
Printed in the USA
FFHW021248241218
49986424-54682FF